Match Fishing Our Way

**Ken Giles and
Clive Smith**

THE ANGLING TIMES
in association with

DAVID & CHARLES
Newton Abbot   London   North Pomfret (Vt)

To Gordon Holland for his help in
preparing the book and to John
Sheward for the drawings

British Library Cataloguing in Publication Data

Giles, Ken
    Match fishing our way.
    1. Tournament fishing
    I. Title II. Smith, Clive   III. Angling times
    799.1'2   SH455.2
    ISBN 0–7153–7692–6

Printed in Great Britain
by Redwood Burn Limited, Trowbridge & Esher
for David & Charles (Publishers) Limited
Brunel House Newton Abbot Devon

Published in the United States of America
by David & Charles Inc
North Pomfret Vermont 05053   USA

Contents

Introduction:
A Sound Approach
to Top Match Fishing

There is no easy, short cut to success in the world of match fishing. It is a long, hard road, full of disappointments and setbacks, and the angler with the temperament and the will to overcome these temporary checks is the one with the best chance of reaching the top.

As with many other facets of life, sporting or otherwise, a sound apprenticeship is essential in the moulding of a first-class matchman. For the raw beginner, angling tuition by qualified instructors is becoming more widely available. This is an excellent means not only of learning how to fish, but also of obtaining knowledge of the various species which are going to be caught. However, even having grasped these basics of the sport, there is still a long way to go before an angler is really fit to enter the competitive side with any hope of success, even at the lowest level.

The first priority is to get the feel of the match scene. And this can be done only by attending good class open events in a spectator role. In the early stages it pays to follow a match through from the draw to the weigh-in because there is much valuable information to be gained.

The angling Press is an excellent guide for the budding matchman to follow in selecting the venues in his area where top anglers are likely to congregate. These will almost certainly be waters where something like a third of the pegs have a winning potential, venues which he himself will choose later on in his career. He can also become familiar with the more consistent names on the circuit. And a question here and there will soon suggest to him the right anglers to watch, and talk to. He should observe exactly how these competitors start a match because the first hour or so of any contest can be vital. It is far more important to note the initial preparation needed to catch fish, than to watch during the actual catching period. This is the time when the contestant is planning the next few hours in his head, ascertaining water depth, strength of flow and general conditions with a view to selecting the right tackle for the swim.

However, this is *not* the right time to start chatting to the competitor, in the hope of gaining a few tips. He is far too busy weighing up his approach to the match. But he can be watched —discreetly, of course, and certainly not from a position right on top of his swim! A word or two to introduce oneself to the matchman should not be objected to, however. And then when he is settled, and has time, he will probably explain his approach and what he hopes to achieve.

A point to watch in these early stages is the feeding pattern. Compare the quantity of bait introduced into the swim with that used later in the match when, for instance, a lot of fish are being caught. Observe, too, the point of entry of the feed and the area where the angler is trying his hardest to catch. These marks differ widely between still water and a moving river.

A top matchman rarely uses all his swim, partly because he likes to work on a run of probably three or four yards where the concentration of fish should be after an hour's feeding. Another point is that if he fishes too far down his swim, he is at the mercy of the competitor below him. He also likes to leave an area as a sort of sanctuary for the fish to drop back into before regaining the confidence to start feeding again later in the match.

It will undoubtedly be noticed that the experienced match angler does not often fish the exact depth of his swim. In the winter months, for instance, his tackle will probably be adjusted to let more line lie on the bottom, and the run-through slowed down to the extent that he may be fishing at, say 7–8ft in a swim with a vertical depth of only 6ft. Take note of his tackle layout, and how quickly he starts to catch. His approach will be neat, efficient, and seemingly unhurried. This is because a top angler's code is, the more haste the less speed.

In open contests certain trends will be seen to be adopted over a period of time, but, in general, the more successful angler is not a trend follower. He likes to make up his own mind. As an example, an angler may fall for a centre-pin reel and use it because it looks more impressive. But he would probably do far better and catch more fish by using an 'easier' type of reel. There are times when the centre-pin has a distinct advantage over other designs, but to use it properly is an art in itself and newcomers to the sport are advised to keep to the more generally accepted types.

Even at the weigh-in there is something to be learned. The top matchmen watch very carefully while their catches are being weighed. Mistakes can be made, even by the most experienced scalesmen, and a mere ounce or two can cost a competitor the match. It will usually be noted, too, how the better class of matchmen use great care in returning their fish to the water. They know that they will be hoping to catch them again at a later date.

The importance of this angler-study can't be over-emphasized. Even having reached international standard, we don't miss an opportunity of going along to watch a contest if we believe that something can be learned. However good a match angler may be, he can always add to his store of knowledge. Ideally, this period of watching the top anglers in action should continue for at least a whole season, and then be maintained during the next term when a few minor club matches could be entered. To plunge into the match scene without this prior groundwork will leave an angler floundering, and is not the way to success. True, it may result in one or two cases of 'beginner's luck', but this never lasts long and, in the present high standard of competition, would inevitably lead to disillusionment, and a possible early retirement from the game.

After the contest, back at headquarters, more useful information can be gained while waiting for the prize presentation. The winner is often generous in giving details of how he fished; what tackle and baits he used. Useful tips can also be obtained from other competitors. There are some anglers, of course, who might say a lot but give little away and the learner will quickly get to know which are the most reliable sources to approach.

Near-at-home venues should be fully assessed before travelling long distances to test out a variety of waters, which can lead the beginner to become a jack of all trades and a master of none. Apart from the high cost of travelling, it is essential for a match angler to concentrate on a venue, realize the moods and true potential of the water, and become proficient at fishing it, before trying other locations. This alone will entail very many visits for practice workouts, and will mean adopting varying methods—there is not a venue in the country which dictates a single method for success.

The successful angler also has to be very much a handyman, especially where floats and hooks are concerned. For instance, the commercial hook-tier cannot be expected to carry out individual greasing of the hooks to eliminate rust on those which remain in the wallet for a period of time. And certain methods necessitate items which cannot be purchased over the counter.

When thinking of acquiring rods and reels it is advisable first to ask around and find out the designs which the top anglers are using. All rods and reels which are intended for use should be interchangeable. It is bad policy, in view of the now generally accepted rule that more than one rod can be set up at a match, to have, say, a bale-arm reel on one rod, and a closed-face type on another.

The budding match angler will no doubt be fascinated by the large assortment of tackle which the expert takes with him to a contest, and the wide variety of baits he sees in use. The whole subject of baits, in fact, is of prime importance, and warrants detailed discussion.

PART ONE
Tackle

1 Rods

Rods

When dealing with the subject of tackle, it is perhaps proper to start with what is generally regarded as the main item among the match angler's equipment—the rod. It is pretty safe to say that of all tackle items, the rod is the one which has remained fundamentally unchanged since the days of Izaak Walton. There have, of course, been modified designs, and new basic materials have been brought into use.

From the cane rods, which reigned for hundreds of years, there was a move to aluminium-alloy tube designs, and we are now well into the era of the fibre-glass rod, with a steadily increasing showing of the carbon-fibre products which will undoubtedly play a significant part in match rods of the future.

We have recently been very much involved in the production of a top match rod and have therefore become familiar with the definitions of a useful tool looked at, so to speak, from both sides of the fence. We were instrumental in totally discarding the staggered ring pattern in favour of small size 'O' rings along the length of the rod, a move which completely broke from tradition.

Dealing first with *float fishing*, all the basic requirements can be fulfilled very adequately with a rod 12–13ft long. Depth of water to be fished has very little relevance to the rod length, it is really just a question of personal choice. And anglers do have varying preferences. In fact, the authors themselves differ in this respect.

We will now give a general breakdown of an efficient match rod, used in conjunction with the ultra-fine tackle which is so popular among top anglers.

13

The key part is the business end of the rod, the top joint, in which maximum efficiency can be obtained only by use of a splice which gives a fine tip with a more meaty middle joint. It should be understood that rods are built on mandrels with a uniform taper. This means that if a match rod was made with a fine tip and this slender taper was carried through the rod, the middle joint would become too sloppy. Conversely, if the middle joint was made on substantial lines, and the same taper was carried through to the tip, then the tip, in turn, would be much too robust.

The purpose of the middle joint is to give power to assist casting. It is also used as a stabilizer in the general balance of the rod, neutralizing the force exerted in either striking or casting. For example, a weak middle joint would lead to vibrations continuing long after the manoeuvre had been completed.

The qualities required of a top joint are such that it should be capable of handling fine 1lb breaking-strain lines with full efficiency and without fear of breakage.

This leaves the butt joint which, in comparison with the other two, is the poor relation. It merely facilitates the holding of the rod, but it is still important that it should be comfortable to hold. A slender butt is essential, around $1\frac{1}{16}$in diameter is ideal, because this allows a good margin of overlap for the fingers, an important factor when maintaining a rhythm over the duration of a contest. It also has better balance and control, giving ample scope for the fingers to be placed on the reel.

Gone are the frills and trappings of the match rod of a few years ago. The screwed-in rubber cap, for instance, which was considered so essential, or the chrome cap at the top of the cork handle. These served no useful purpose whatsoever and merely helped to weigh down the rod. Coupled with the fact that the ferrules used to be of metal, it can easily be seen that an angler had to carry a lot of unnecessary weight. These ferrules have now been replaced by glass-to-glass spigot designs which are far superior to the male and female types as they do not demand that the rod should increase in diameter at each ferrule.

However, there is no real substitute for the cork handle, which has for long been so reliable. Its advantages are numerous, not the least being its amazing capacity to absorb all forms of moist-

14

ure. As can be imagined, this is invaluable on wet days. And equally important, it effectively neutralizes other tacky substances which would work against a good firm grip on the rod. The cork can be an advantage, too, in extremely cold conditions, as it always seems warmer to the hand than other materials.

There is a very good reason for the incorporation in the rod of all size 'O' rings. In fact, it might shock many to know the weight saving which is obtained by their substitution. For instance, an intermediate rod ring comprises about 7in of wire gauge, as against 3½in for the size 'O' ring—twice as much! And there is a further saving of a ten-thousandth of an inch on the wire gauge between a size 'O' and an intermediate ring. The total weight saved is therefore considerable when it is realized that there are nine rings on a 12ft rod.

Although there can never be one weight of rod which is ideal for every angler, it is true to say that about 90 per cent will opt for a rod in the 8–10oz range. It is, of course, entirely a matter of personal choice.

It is important, when selecting a rod and finding one to suit personal requirements, to stay with that particular design. With most present-day match rules permitting the setting up of more than one rod, it is a distinct disadvantage to have to switch from one model to another during a contest. This completely destroys rhythm.

With all the teething troubles now ironed out, fibre-glass rods are enjoying their full potential. Carbon-fibre designs are comparatively new on the market and it will probably take another five or six years before these are fully accepted.

Leger rods take two forms, *quiver-tip* or *swing-tip*. And while most anglers make do with one swing-tip, several top joints to the quiver-tip rod will be needed to cover all contingencies. The right tip to use is, of course, determined by the pace of the water being fished, and this range of tips is best fashioned to suit personal requirements. Although tips have been produced in spring steel and other similar materials, we find that glass is the only really suitable material. It is advisable to buy it ready ground if possible, rather than having to fashion it yourself, as the forces are thus distributed evenly.

Legering can be looked upon as a sort of thermometer—still

water at the base with a zero rating, and fast water at the top of the chart. If the lower range is the swing-tip, then come varying degrees of quiver-tips to the most robust design at the top for the fast-running swims. Rarely will an angler need the full complement of tips. It will, of course, depend largely on the area in which he lives and does his fishing. For instance, a North Country angler will need tips to suit the harder-running rivers of the Yorkshire Dales, as will the Midlander fishing the equally strong-flowing Wye and Severn. They will settle for a trio of tips of the more robust pattern. For the Fenland angler, however, more used to moderate-flowing rivers and broads, finer quiver-tips at the lower end of the scale, or a swing-tip, would be the answer.

In the preparation of a swing-tip it is essential, in order to avoid tangles when casting, that the distance between the tip end and the top joint of the rod should be kept to a minimum, not greater than $\frac{3}{16}$in. Generally speaking, the length of the tip can best be summed up by following the practice, the stiller the water the longer the tip. It can be argued that the longer tip is the more sensitive, but, ideally, if an angler starts with a tip around 9in long, after practice and experience, personal preference will eventually take over.

As a joining medium from the tip end to the top joint of the rod, rubber of very soft texture should be used to make the 'hinge'.

In leger fishing a bite is indicated by movement of the tip which is, in effect, the float. And, as with a float, it is necessary to paint only a very small area, say an inch, and not, as the reader has probably often seen, up to a foot of zebra-like stripes extending up the rod. This can be very trying on the eyes.

Although there are limited uses for the very short quiver-tip rod, known as the wand, which is really a specialist tool, the length of both quiver-tip and swing-tip rods tends to be in the 9ft plus bracket. This again is really a matter of personal choice.

A swing-tipping rod is correctly associated with bream, although there are one or two exceptions to this, for example, the carp of the North Country canals. The rod must be tailor-made to suit the soft-mouthed bream. It will not be of tip-action design, but of a more even nature. In fact, in terms of a float-fishing rod it would probably be described as of 'sloppy' construction. It is a soft-action rod, having the basic requirements of being able to absorb the slow, lunging action of the bream, with the middle joint being the all-important section.

Whilst, with a match rod, a careful balance between the number of rings and the weight has to be achieved so as not to destroy the action of the rod, this does not apply with the leger rod where the balance factor does not assume the same importance, and so more rings can be used. Indeed, they are necessary to assist the line to follow the curve of the rod, an important factor when playing a fish, without risk of the hook pulling free, which often happens with a more solid type of rod. With leger rods, lowbell rings are commonly used.

The butt is equal in requirement with the leger rod as with other types. The main requisite is a nice comfortable handle, ideally of cork material, but the length is usually a little shorter on the leger rod, about $\frac{4}{5}$ of that on the float rod.

In more recent years, assisted largely by changing rules, *swimfeeder fishing*, at one time confined mainly to the southern part of the country, has become a more nationally accepted method. This requires a special rod, particularly when fishing fast-flowing rivers.

The feeder has to be anchored in the middle of the river and, having quite a large cross-sectional area, can easily be moved by a strong current. To help to secure his position, the feeder angler often brings into use one or two $\frac{1}{2}$in bullets. This is in addition to the lead strip built into the feeder, plus the maggots and groundbait which it contains.

It is, therefore, not difficult to see that a substantial rod is required for this type of fishing, probably on the lines of the tackle used by the carp or salmon angler. A standard leger rod length of around 9ft is quite suitable, and there is little need for a quiver-tip or other bite-detection aid. For reasons best known to the fish, they seem almost suicidal in their efforts to get on the hook in this type of angling. In fact, a quiver-tip can be a big handicap, as breakage will undoubtedly occur when trying to cast the substantial weight referred to.

There are differing views about the most suitable colour for a rod. Some anglers favour the theory that a lightish colour is hardly seen from beneath the water, while others say that a dark object is less frightening to the fish. We tend to take the middle view and go for a blended colour like mahogany-brown.

Poles

Through the medium of the World Championship and other cross-Channel visits, our friends on the Continent have, in more recent years, introduced us to the use of the pole in match fishing. Some anglers in this country, top-class matchmen among them, would have us believe that these poles are the be-all and end-all of match fishing, and the sooner we throw away our other rods, the better we will all be for it. This we certainly do not go along with. We view the pole as a necessary item of tackle, but very limited in its use.

One fact alone can explain why Continentals totally accept the pole, yet the British angler is reluctant to use it, and that is the big difference in the length of matches. Across the Channel the duration of contests varies from as little as thirty minutes to a more standard period of ninety. In fact, their argument about the World Championship, a three-hour match, is that it is to them more of a marathon! The British matchman is used to fishing matches of four or five hours. And there are not many Continentals who would cherish the thought of fishing a five-hour match using a 28–30ft pole!

However, the pole does have its uses in our matches. It is unbeatable with certain types of canal work, and also in most situations when bleak fishing. Telescopic poles were first got off the ground by the British angler, but these are now rapidly being substituted with take-apart types. The advantages are enormous – these poles can easily be extended by adding sections when required, and this can be invaluable when a large fish is encountered and the extra length is needed to play it.

The two main types of fishing in which we see the pole playing its part are angling for small fish in still waters, and bleak fishing. Every angler knows the type of venue we mean when talking about the former. There are so many waters in this country, mostly canals, where species like gudgeon form the basis of a winning catch. At the same time it is always on the cards that the odd big fish will be encountered, and these can prove vital in matches where two or three pounds are usually sufficient to win.

To safeguard against losing these better fish, it is advisable to incorporate a *crook attachment* in the pole set-up. This comprises a length of rubber and a wire crook. The rubber is attached to the line at one end (see Fig 1) and to the crook at the other end, and acts simply as a shock absorber to prevent line breakage. Varying strengths of rubber are available, fine, medium, and heavy, and it is best used in lengths of 6–7in.

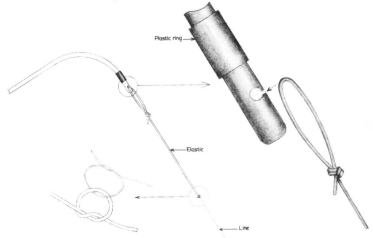

Fig 1 (right) Fit elastic loop into slot, then cover with plastic ring; (left) tie elastic into one loop knot. Pass line through and tie one loop knot. Pull both elastic and line knots together tightly—then pull elastic inside out and trim

When fishing for bleak, the pole has distinct advantages when fish are numerous. It is best used in conjunction with a solid glass tip approximating the specifications of a quiver-tip. And as there is little chance of any large fish being encountered in this style of fishing, the use of elastic can be dispensed with, as it may prove more of a hindrance than a help.

As regards other uses of the pole, there can be possible advantages in flood conditions when holding out in the stream with light float tackle helps to catch fish. But the angler should be very wary that a specimen of large proportions—often so important if landed in these sort of conditions—can be lost because of the limitations of the pole. Although we don't entirely rule out this method, one should be very sure that the chances of coming across bigger fish are negligible, and this is not a situation which can apply to many venues.

As with bleak fishing, the pole could be an ideal method for dace. But there is again the same question mark against its use. The plain fact is, there are very few venues in this country where one can be sure of encountering dace alone. Invariably, the companion of the dace is the chub!

Clive Smith slides a fish into his net

2 Reels

The budding matchman will very quickly realize that he has to make a harrowing choice when it comes to reels—the once highly popular *centre-pin* type, the *open-face* variety, or the *close-face* design which, during the past few years, has gained more and more affection among the match-angling fraternity.

Turning first to the centre-pin, we would not advise the angler to get involved too much with this particular type. To use it efficiently is an art all on its own. In years gone by this was the only type available and complete dedication was needed to make the tackle perform to its full potential.

Now, things are far different as, with the open- and close-face patterns taking over, the dilemma of the centre-pin is removed. The authors both started their fishing with the centre-pin, in fact, and have travelled the somewhat tricky road of endeavour before now coming, with some relief, to the position where the close-face job does almost everything they could wish.

The open-face reel was the natural successor to the centre-pin and what a wonderful servant it has been to the angler. Its main advantage was to create a 'no limit' situation regarding casting distance. Overnight, as it were, the far side of the river became the angler's territory, instead of merely the near margin, as had previously been the case. Legering, too, now became a distinct method of fishing, and must owe its emergence to the open-face reel.

There was still one big disadvantage, however, both with the centre-pin and the open-face design : they necessitated the use of both hands when recasting. And it was the realization of this shortcoming that led very shortly to another model being launched onto the market, one which allowed for the operation to be carried out single-handed. This was the now vastly popular close-face design.

This is not to say that we have seen the last of the open-face type. Indeed, for heavy-line fishing, notably in the field of swim-feeders, this model still reigns supreme.

The close-face reel has many advantages, not the least being its sheer simplicity of use. A lot of thought was put into the design to ensure comfortable, fingertip control, so vastly important when fishing moving water. It also does away with the more complex bale-arm mechanism of the open-face design and the extra weight involved, substituting a much simpler mechanism, and this has resulted in an ideally weighted and balanced product.

By eliminating the bale-arm it also left the way open for a completely new design of pick-up, the stud type. This requires only a fraction of the material and created what is now known as the instant pick-up. It was achieved by the immediate 'pop-up' action of the stud, replacing the 180-degree travelling distance of the old mouse-trap bale-arm, and with it the unavoidable momentary slackening of the line prior to engagement with the bale-arm.

As its name might suggest, the close-face reel is ideally suited to windy conditions. Its protective casing fully encloses the line, thus preventing any disturbance to its efficient working. As in the case of the rod, we have been closely associated with the design of a close-face reel, and, in our model, have taken a step away from tradition. Gone is the star-drag-type slipping clutch, often so inconsistent and adversely affected by the elements. We believe there is only one way, and that is complete manual control. All we require of a reel are two factors—to wind forward, and to wind back.

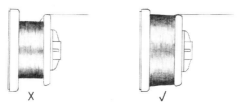

Fig 2 Right and wrong way of filling spools

One other difference between the close- and open-face reels is the recommended loading of the spools. With the open type it is advisable to load the line to within $\frac{1}{16}$in of the lip. This lessens the friction created as the line leaves the spool (see Fig 2). With the close-face type, however, the line leaves the spool vertically, instead of horizontally, and in this case it is not advantageous to load the spool quite so fully.

3 Floats

Among all the items of tackle, the float is the one which is possibly the most misunderstood. There are literally thousands of different designs, some more popular than others, and each model invariably comes in seven or eight sizes. It can well be imagined that to the budding matchman this must cause an almost insurmountable problem in the early stages of his career. It is often said, in fact, that floats catch more anglers than fish, and, unfortunately, this is very true. As with most avenues of angling, the correct choice and use of floats comes largely with experience.

Inevitably, the popularity of the various types of float varies in different parts of the country. While the *stick float* is widely respected for use in the Midlands on the faster-flowing waters such as the Trent and Severn, it is the *antenna* type which gets the vote in the Fenland areas.

The stick float is undoubtedly the most popular type for use in moving waters. Its origin stems largely from the North Country anglers who devised it in the early 1960s for their frequent visits to the Trent, at a time when large catches were commonplace. A big proportion of these catches was taken 'on the drop', even in winter time. This was attributable, in large measure, to the unnaturally high water temperatures brought about by power stations along the river, which led to the fish being encouraged to feed at depths well off the riverbed, and so the need arose for a float which would indicate bites at all levels. The stick float was the answer.

It is made of two types of wood, differing largely in density. Ideally, balsa wood forms the upper part of the float and constitutes about a third of its length. This is one of the most buoyant

24

types of wood known to the angler. The lower part of the float, making up the other two-thirds, consists of a very hard wood, barely buoyant, such as the outer casing of a bamboo cane. This larger part assists casting greatly, and, although the shotting capacity of a stick float may be only 2BB, it has distance capabilities equal to a 4BB or 5BB all-balsa or quill float.

To achieve this situation of bite indication at all depths, the stick float must be fixed double-rubber, and the shotting pattern should be as illustrated in Fig 3. It is then equally important that the tackle is cast out onto the water, as shown in Fig 4.

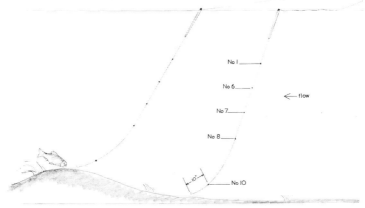

No 1

No 6

←— flow

No 7

No 8

10"   No 10

Fig 3 The set-up shown is for approx 6ft depth of water. All shot equally spaced. Add one No 1 shot for every extra foot of water

It cannot be over-emphasized that when working with a stick float, a bad cast, resulting in the wrong formation of the tackle on the water, can never be remedied during the swim down. It is best to retrieve the line and start again. This is why the budding matchman should study Fig 4 very carefully and make sure it is followed to the letter.

A position has now been reached where the tackle is in the water, correctly shotted, and in a position as illustrated in Fig 3. Because of its special design, the float will now clearly indicate any bite which comes as the hook bait travels down from the surface to the bed of the river. A clearer picture of this can be seen in Fig 5.

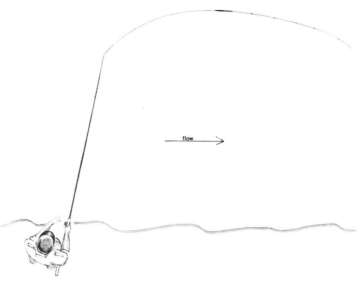

Fig 4 Laying tackle on water correctly

Going back to Fig 3, it will be noticed that the shots are graded, with the smallest size nearest the hook, and becoming larger as they approach the float. This is done to aid presentation. The sort of swims where this float is used often have very uneven bottoms, perhaps 6–7ft at the top of the swim, shelving

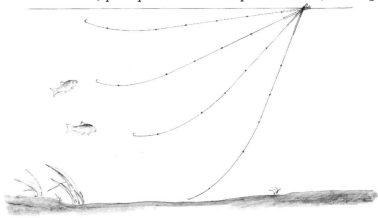

Fig 5 Correct action of stick float set up

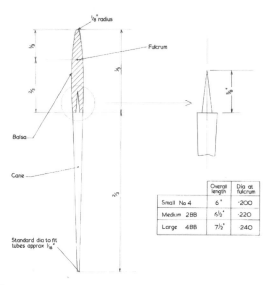

	Overall length	Dia at fulcrum
Small No 4	6"	·200
Medium 2BB	6½"	·220
Large 4BB	7½"	·240

Fig 6a Shot capacity can vary fractionally on above dimensions owing to the density of balsa wood

to 5ft half-way down, then deepening again to 7ft at the down-stream end. By applying strain to the float, the hook can be made to lift at the required spot down the swim, then lowered again when necessary by easing the strain (see Fig 3). If the tackle was shotted too heavily at the bottom, this would not be possible.

In this way the bait can be presented much more naturally, because when pressure is applied it is slowed to an ideal speed, thus simulating a bait free of the hook. We tend to think that, with the aid of friction of the riverbed, this travels at two-thirds the speed of the current. With this method an attractive lift of the bait can be achieved and, as more expertise is gained with this delicate tackle combination, other little tricks become possible.

Floats designed for attaching to the line at both ends have long since dispensed with the fixed ring at the bottom. This has been replaced by a thin-walled plastic tube, similar to a ball-point pen refill, in lengths of $\frac{1}{2}$in. The top attaching aid is the valve-rubber-type of fixer, positioned high up the float in order to leave a dimple of something like $\frac{3}{32}$in visible above the rubber.

27

Top-class stick floats can be purchased from tackle shops but, of course, many anglers find satisfaction in making their own. Fig 6a might be helpful in showing the correct jointing of the two materials involved, and the shape which we have found to work most efficiently.

It is advisable to get together a comprehensive range of stick floats, and a collection of five varying sizes, between the shotting capacity of three No 4 and 4 BB would be ideal. It is recommended that these be either purchased or made in sets of three, as this does ensure that replacements are readily available in case of loss or breakage.

Fig 6b The balsa float is the same shape as the stick with slight adjustment. The dome at the tip of the float starts at ⅛in diameter in small sizes and up to ¼in in larger models. At the base end of the Float a cane insert is fitted for securing the bottom 'rubber' to. To carry the extra shot the diameter can increase by as much ⅜in on larger models

Turning now to the *balsa float* (see Fig 6b) which, to us, is traditional and a regular standby. This is a float which will invariably get the angler out of trouble when fishing the more awkward waters such as the Wye, Hampshire Avon, and fast-flowing Yorkshire waters. The balsa float lends itself to a pattern of bulk shotting, as given in Fig 7. It has somewhat cruder uses than the more sophisticated stick float, and is ideal in bread fishing where the bulk shotting is excellent for depositing a buoyant bait on the bed of a fast-flowing river when the spread-shot pattern of the stick float would be of no use at all.

The shotting capacity of the balsa float takes over somewhere around the point the stick float leaves off, at 4BB, and it is well capable of achieving heavyweight proportions—we have known top Severn anglers go as heavy as seven and eight swans, with excellent results. In terms of shot capacity it is, in fact, the 'heavy' in the armoury of floats.

As in the case of the stick variety, the balsa float is fished 'double rubber'. The same bottom attachment can be used, provided that a standard-size piece of hard cane is inserted into the base of the float. This needs to penetrate only $\frac{5}{8}$in. Whereas the dome of the stick float is $\frac{1}{8}$in in radius, ideally the balsa should have a blunter finish in varying degrees according to its size. Good balsa floats can be purchased, but for home-made articles the softest balsa wood obtainable should be used.

These floats cannot be categorized in sizes like the stick float. An angler will invariably be familiar with the particular water

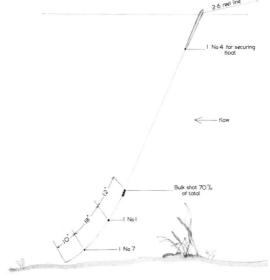

Fig 7 Bulk shot depends on depth and casting distance, ie 7ft of water 3 rod lengths out 6BB

he fishes, and will fashion a float to suit the venue. The range cannot be limited and, in fact, the angler who fishes waters requiring a balsa float will probably finish up with forty or fifty of them among his tackle!

The *slider float*, most commonly used in moving water, is simply a balsa float fitted with a sliding attachment to enable an angler to fish water having a depth far in excess of the length of the rod. With these designs, the shot-carrying capacity starts around $2\frac{1}{2}$ swan. Anything less than this does not work efficiently and it can create a position where the float is propelled backwards by the action of the line running through the guides on it.

To the best of our knowledge, a good slider float, suitable for running water, is not obtainable in the shops. There are sliders which are made for this sort of use, but they fall sadly short of what is required, mainly through the design of the sliding rings which are simply not strong enough to stand up to the hard usage this type of float has to undergo.

The bottom guide is the most vulnerable. The fault here lies in the fact that the bulk shot, moving up fast on the retrieve, tends to hit hard against the ring, which becomes damaged and bends over in a very short time. And though it can be straightened easily enough, it is soon weakened into uselessness. The way round this is to take a small piece of hollow glass-fibre, similar to that at the end of the top joint on a match rod, and cut it into sections of about $\frac{1}{2}$in. Using an engineer's file, two flat lugs of approximately $\frac{1}{8}$in, one at each end, are shaped on the glass; these are for whipping the attachment to the float (see Fig 8).

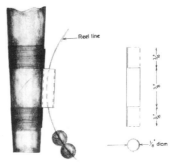

Fig 8 Glass adapter for heavy duty slider

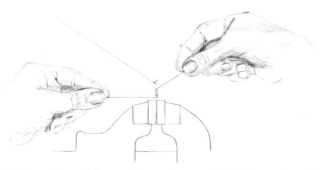

Fig 9a Using either ¹⁄₆₄in needle or silver steel held in a vice. Wrap

This will resist any amount of force caused by the bulk shot.

At the other end of the float there is a ring which is responsible for setting the depth and ensuring a clean strike. Here again, commercial floats fall down on both requirements. To achieve a clean strike the ring should be placed as near to the tip of the float as possible, enabling the line to float on the surface of the water in the same way as with a stick float. If the ring is positioned too far down the float, it tends to submerge the line, and makes a clean strike very difficult. Another point is that when any mending of the line is needed, as it very often is in top and bottom float fishing in moving water, it becomes very hard, if not quite impossible, with a submerged line. The make-up of this ring is important, and a close look at Figs 9a–9b will give guidance on this point.

For the shotting of this float, a standard pattern is given in Fig 9b.

It is not necessary to acquire a large range of slider floats. A set somewhere around four swans will accommodate most waters. This is an ideal weight at which the slider works efficiently, and we have yet to find a swim which cannot be fished quite competently with this size.

All the floats so far dealt with have been *double rubber* designs, that is, attached to the line at both ends. We now come to a float with a different type of attachment, the *waggler*. As its name might suggest, it is fixed to the line at one end only—via the bottom ring.

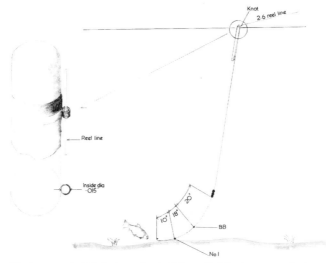

Fig 9b (top and right) Attached slider; (left) close-up of ring

Until the early 1970s it was considered wrong to fish moving water by this bottom ring style, but the waggler has changed all that. It has, in fact, gained such popularity as to be considered an essential tool in the matchman's float box.

It is no coincidence that the emergence of this float has come with the chub explosion. It offers the finest possible bait presentation to the chub and it can be cast long distances with great accuracy. Most important, too, the light shotting pattern, essential to the style of fishing for which it is used, can be adopted without the risk of tangles so commonplace when fishing double rubber style at long distances.

It didn't take long for anglers to realize the potential of this float in catching other species apart from chub. This was proved most effectively on rivers like the Trent where, during the 'dry' years, it was extended from a normal summer and autumn method to be used throughout the season.

Unlike the stick float, the waggler is one of the simplest floats to make. It can be bought over the counter, although difficulty might be experienced in obtaining the larger sizes due to shortage of materials. Basically, a float can be made from either

peacock or sarkandass reed and in most cases the latter is preferred, especially in conditions of strong winds, when a better
flight can be achieved. This does not mean that the peacock
variety doesn't have its day too. It comes into its own more
particularly in turbulent conditions where extra buoyancy is
needed.

There is really little use for a waggler float of a size less than,
say, 2AAA, and, starting at this capacity, a range would extend
up to shot-carrying proportions of 4 swan. The heavier designs
will probably have to incorporate balsa or cork bodies to make
up the required bulk of the float, because it is difficult to obtain
either peacock or sarkandass of sufficient proportions. This will,
of course, entail an additional operation in fitting the body.

For the smaller sizes, all that is needed is a length of either
reed or quill, whichever is preferred. The lengths will vary between 6in and about 10in, and the diameter will be geared to
accommodate the varying shotting sizes required. It is essential
to obtain a correct balance between length and diameter to avoid
spiralling of the float on casting, caused by too much length
being used. For floats which are required to work in all but the
most turbulent waters, a top insert, in the same material, will
be required. This is to lessen the resistance felt by the fish when
it accepts the bait and can vary in size between $\frac{1}{16}$–$\frac{1}{8}$in diameter.
It is usually about 2in long and is simply slotted about $\frac{1}{2}$in
down into the main stem of the float and permanently fixed.

At the base of the float another insert has to be fixed by the
same method, this one made of hard cane and protruding $\frac{1}{2}$in
from the main body. The purpose of this is merely to accept
the adapter, now widely used for fixing the waggler, in place of
the bottom ring. If the insert is tapered slightly with a file or
grinder before fixing, this will assist with the fitting of the
adapter.

This adapter, shown in Fig 10, is simply a short length of
hard plastic tube, with an outside diameter of about $\frac{1}{8}$in, which
acts as a removable bottom ring to the float. Obviously, the diameter of the insert must be the same on all floats for the purpose
of interchangeability, so often the key to success.

Turning to the heavier, cork-bodied or balsa-bodied design,
the shape of this is important in terms of resistance. From the

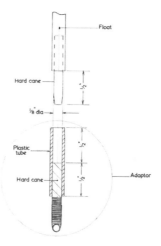

Fig 10 Float adapter

sketch given in Fig 11, it can be seen that the taper is at the base of the float. The reason for this is fairly obvious when considering how the float will act on the strike and on its travels through the water.

When fishing with a waggler, the overhead method of casting is recommended whenever possible. It is by far the most accurate, and will result in fewer tangles with the ultra-light shotting pattern in use.

At the required distance, in order to trim the tackle, pressure should be applied to the spool of the reel, and this will lay the tackle on the water in a straight line. As we are dealing with moving water, a good tip here is always to cast downstream, somewhere in the region of 2 o'clock. Invariably, the waggler method is used for fishing well across the river towards the far bank and, in most cases, the faster water is at mid-river. This tends to drag the line round, thus pulling the float at a greater speed than the current at that point where it is actually situated and the downstream cast will help to obviate this.

This situation is exaggerated when there is a downstream wind and many anglers are left struggling because they do not make full use of this manoeuvre to overcome the problem.

To give an instance of this tactic, when fishing a match on

the Warwickshire Avon at Fladbury, a popular Midlands venue, conditions were very similar to those mentioned, and we enjoyed 100 per cent success by taking the top two places.

There was a gale force wind, and we were pegged at opposite ends of the match course and although this stretch does bend a little, by far the majority of competitors find themselves with the wind operating in the same direction.

Knowledge and carrying out of this downstream angle casting manoeuvre not only enabled us to finish first and second but made it a comparatively easy match for us to fish, despite the fact that the majority of the field were floundering, trying to cope with the very difficult conditions.

As mentioned previously, this tackle is often fished at ranges of 30–35yds, and, in a situation like this, the more assistance which can be gained with casting, the better. This is why the positioning of the shots is so important. The bulk of the shot, something like 80 per cent, is placed on either side of the float, leaving a gap of about ⅜in for manoeuvrability and to eliminate line breakage. The remaining shots are positioned at intervals down the line so as to give the attractive presentation of the bait

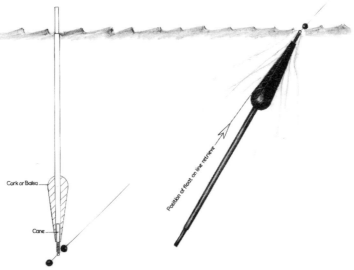

Cork or Balsa

Cane

Position of float on line retrieve

Fig 11 Bottom-attached float leaving water

35

Ken Giles draws a fish to hand : his unorthodox hold on the rod is due to the excessive depth of water

which is so important when fishing for chub. Either a micro-dust, or a dust shot, depending on the species, is placed 12–18in away from the hook. This distance varies and is dependent upon two factors. Firstly, the nature of the riverbed has to be taken into consideration : the cleaner this is, then the nearer to the hook can the shot be placed. The second factor involves the tendency of the fish to rise or chase the bait. The more active the fish, then the greater the distance between the hook and the shot.

Working further away from the hook, the distance between this first shot and the next one along the line is a little greater than that between the hook and the first shot. Depending on the selected size of the initial shot, this second lead should be the next largest size, then a No 4 should be added roughly half-way between this second shot and the float.

This shotting pattern will work admirably in depths up to 8–9ft. Depths greater than this will usually require the addition of a No 1 shot for each extra 2ft of water. This can be placed some 2ft below the float. For clarification of this shotting pattern, see Fig 12.

There is a noticeable difference between the waggler and the stick float: the waggler rides proud of the water by a far greater amount. The reason for this is quite simple really. With the stick float, pressure can be applied to lift the hook over an uneven or snaggy riverbed, but this is almost impossible with the waggler, and assistance must be forthcoming from the float itself. The more buoyant, high-riding waggler serves to do this very well indeed.

The introduction of the points system in the National Championship made it desirable, if not essential, for the match angler to be competent at catching bleak. The floats needed for this type of work complete our recommended range of floats for moving water.

Basically, two types are needed for bleak fishing, one for surface work and the other for taking fish at varying depths. The latter is, of course, mostly applicable to the winter months. The

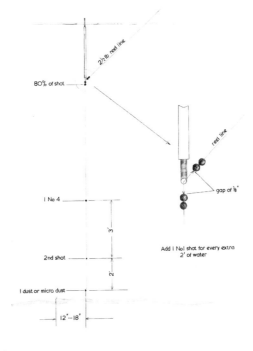

Fig 12 Waggler set-up

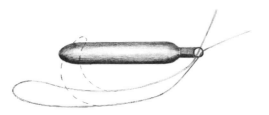

Fig 13 Surface float : how to secure to line

definitions of the two floats are completely different. Summer tactics dictate that the float is merely to assist casting and has no use whatever as a bite indicator. For winter fishing, however, the float has a more orthodox use in registering bites in the normal way.

Bleak invariably feed on or very near the surface in the summer period, and, if an angler worked to the normal method of float bite indication, this would be far too slow for him to be able to finish with anything like a competitive weight. Instead, bite detection is made simply by observing the movement of the line between the hook and the float.

This is dealt with more fully in the chapter dealing with bleak fishing, but it is important at this stage to appreciate the correct function of the float. As purely an aid to casting, it has obviously to be made of a material containing the required properties, and it is essential, too, that it should have a low water profile to lessen wind trouble. We have found the ideal material to be beech wood.

This float should not be painted or varnished, the idea being to allow it to absorb water, thus giving it more weight to assist casting. A range of floats to cover all requirements should include sizes from $1\frac{1}{2}$in long and $\frac{3}{16}$in diameter to somewhere around $2\frac{1}{2}$in long and $\frac{1}{4}$in diameter. A ring can be fitted to one end for attachment, as it is far better to fish waggler style to avoid tangles as much as possible.

Obviously, when fishing the surface, the addition of any shots to lock the float would simply defeat the purpose. Attachment to the line should be made by the loop method, as described in Fig. 13.

During the winter months, a contest often has to be fished

38

in very poor conditions where, say, two or three pounds can be enough to win a match. This is where bleak tend to play a much bigger role. They can often be found at depths of 3–4ft, and, from our experience, the ideal float is the porcupine quill. Its properties are well suited to negotiate turbulent conditions. A recommended range of these 'porkies' would be between 2BB and 4BB, with the bulk of the shot situated on either side of the float and one No 8 down the line to aid presentation.

Turning now to still waters, the swing-tip and quiver-tip have played the major roles in recent years, but the match angler must still be aware of the great necessity of being equipped with the right float on the right day.

The swing-tip has been largely responsible for the removal of the larger type of float from the still-water scene, although this is not completely the case. There are still important roles which this float alone can play. But, with roach becoming more prominent again, it is probably fair to say that a smaller float is realizing a greater potential, season by season.

With very few exceptions, floats used for still-water fishing are bottom attached only. When summer or autumn fishing for skimmer bream, or roach, say, up to the 1lb mark, a float is by far superior to the more static method of swing-tipping, although the latter will prove unbeatable for the larger shoaling bream in the 2–3lb class.

For large expanses of water, a float in the category of 3–4 swans is often needed, and at weights like these it is essential that a body is incorporated in the build of the float. To accommodate these capacities, lengths of either peacock or sarkandass reed would be out of all proportion and would not lend to consistency in flight when long casting.

This float may seem similar to its counterpart for moving waters, but where it differs mainly is in its length. A much longer design is often needed to deal with the far greater surface disturbance encountered on the large expanses of water where it will be used. It is not uncommon to have surface movement up to 18in in depth. It is obvious from this that the body must be situated at the lower end of the float in order to avoid unnatural movement of the bait.

A range of these floats going up to 5 swans will be required,

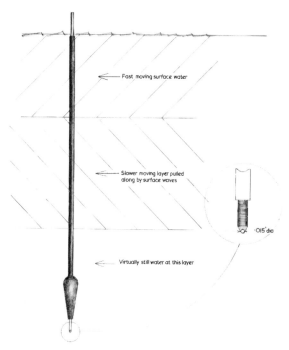

Fast moving surface water

Slower moving layer pulled
along by surface waves

·015˝dia

Virtually still water at this layer

Fig 14 The length of the float is selected so as to situate body of float in a still layer of water. Float could be up to 18in in length in exceptional conditions

and here again the materials best suited are sarkandass reed or peacock, with an insert of the same material, and a body of balsa wood or cork. A proportional diagram is given for guidance in the make-up of the float (see Fig 14).

A useful tip is to select a slider-type adapter with a small-bore ring, as the float is then suitable for both slider and fixed methods. This can be most useful as it is never certain when a switch from one style to another might be profitable.

The shotting pattern for fixed float fishing is pretty well identical to that for the moving water waggler. For depths in excess of 12–13ft, we would strongly advise the use of a sliding float. Many anglers seem reluctant to use this rig and would much prefer to struggle against the odds with fixed float tackle. The best solution to this dilemma is simply to ignore that the float is sliding and treat this style in the normal fashion.

With the slider, however, a completely different shotting pattern is required, and this is given in the accompanying diagram, Fig 15. Also illustrated is the best way of tying a sliding knot.

When fishing large areas of water it can often be helpful if the colour of the float can be changed at a moment's notice. A red tip might be ideal at the start of a match, but surface disturbance can bring about conditions where a black tip is absolutely essential. This can be accomplished very easily by taking a piece of black insulating tape and just wrapping it round the float tip.

A float which has enjoyed great success over the past few seasons is the waggler in the 3AAA– 4AAA bracket. This has developed in tune with the ever-increasing catches of roach during the winter months, notably on the Welland and the Witham. It is comparable almost entirely with its moving-water counterpart of the same size, with one exception – the length of

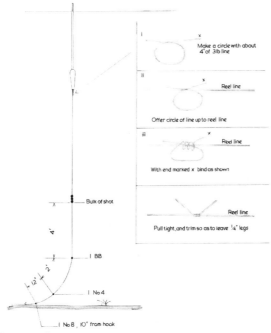

Fig 15 Bottom ring slider

the insert. For the still-water variety this is much longer and can be from a fifth of the total length of the float up to even half of its size. The shotting pattern is in line with that used for the moving-water waggler.

The final port of call in terms of still-water floats concerns the many canals up and down the country. Here again, simplicity is the keyword and, despite many opinions to the contrary, we are prepared to stick our necks out and say that a vast range of floats is not necessary in order to become competent at canal fishing. There are two distinct methods of fishing a canal, with a rod or with a pole. It is probably the most sensitive form of fishing and, although with rod tackle, float, assembly and shotting is carried out on the towpath, it is much better to keep pole tackles on line wrappers.

By far the most common canal float used with a rod is the dart, fished bottom ring only. This is best suited to fishing the far shelf of the canal and seeking the classier fish. It is ideally suited to bread punch, caster, or maggot fishing and can be worked at all depths, from well on the bottom to barely depth.

It is not an easy float to make. The type we prefer has the cane going through the entire length with a skin of balsa wood covering all but the last inch or so at each end. An ideal length is about 5in, and it has a varying shotting pattern according to the thickness of the balsa skin. The cane stem is $\frac{1}{8}$in, fining down considerably at the tip to something like $\frac{1}{16}$in diameter.

When making this float, the most difficult part is to ensure that the balsa skin is firmly attached to the cane throughout its length. If this is not done, it will probbaly come apart during later stages of production. One way of making sure that it is firmly attached is to cut the balsa into small sections, say $\frac{3}{4}$in, and fix each section separately. The sections should be properly mitred and ample time allowed for the glue to set. There is no short cut to fashioning this float; it is a long and laborious job. But the trouble taken can be well worth while as there is no other float to compare with it for the job it is intended to do. Fig 16 gives a little guidance on its manufacture.

We are against the practice of lead-loading of all types of float as we are very much aware of the penetration created by such designs which can often be very disturbing to fish, especially

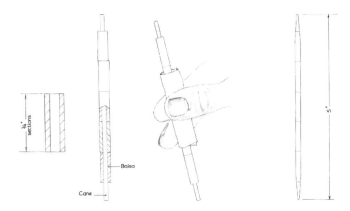

Fig 16 Rub down with fine glass paper

in shallower waters. For some reason which cannot be explained, shots placed at each side of the float do not cause anything like the same disturbance. Shotting patterns depend very much on the movement of water in the canal. Often all that is required is one very small shot, such as a size 10, placed 10–12in from the hook with the float set so that the tackle is 4in on the bottom. This will cope admirably with either a static or slow-moving canal.

The same float can be used, too, where there is more movement, but it is often essential to extend the distance between the float and the hook, so leaving as much as 2ft on the bottom. An extra small shot can be brought down and placed 6–8in above the original shot and this will assist in securing the terminal tackle to the canal bed.

Floats used in conjunction with a pole can be numerous. We have all seen the beautifully turned-out jobs arriving from the Continent. They can be very tempting. These are very new to the British angler and it is well worth remembering the cliché quoted at the start of this chapter, that a float will often catch more anglers than fish.

After lengthy trial and experiment, backed up with some very satisfying match results, we have found that the field of pole floats can be narrowed down to one simple porcupine model. Starting at 1in in length and probably carrying two No

10 shots, it progresses to sizes carrying the equivalent of two No 1's, and these floats are fished in a sophisticated style of double rubber.

A very fine plastic tube is used for attaching to the base of the float, with a nylon loop situated $\frac{1}{4}$in from the tip for the other attachment. To secure this nylon ring, a hot needle is used to penetrate the quill in order that two thicknesses of line can be drawn through. Sufficient line should be left to form a loop, it should be glued in position with Araldite, then trimmed at the back.

The shotting method for this float is invariably round the hook, the bulk of the lead being situated anywhere between 2–6in from it. This tackle is best suited to bloodworm fishing, but it can also be very effective for squatts or other small bait tactics.

4 Hooks

There is only one item of tackle among the angler's 'armoury' without which the catching of fish would be impossible—the hook. From this fact alone, its great importance and the responsibility attached to it can be appreciated.

It has been mentioned previously, when discussing floats, that a big problem is caused by the vast quantity available on the market. Only a small percentage of these can really be recommended as efficient. In no lesser degree this same problem applies to hooks. The varying models and designs run into thousands, and from these the aspiring matchman has to make his choice.

Much has been written about hooks and they have come in for a lot of criticism. This has not been without foundation, because a large majority of the hooks for sale are totally inadequate for the job they are meant to do. To cater for all matchfishing eventualities the field can, in fact, be narrowed down to a mere four models, two in the *forged* variety and two in the *fine-wire* pattern.

In the forged field we have settled for a medium-shank, crystal-bend hook for the larger, powerful fish such as chub and barbel, while for bream in the larger match class of 2–3lb, we recommend a short-shank forged hook of the round-bend pattern. The fine-wire hook we recommend is similar to the first mentioned forged type. This we tend to employ in sizes up to 16, and on odd occasions perhaps 14, in the more placid waters when seeking roach, dace and the occasional chub.

This choice of hook can be something of an obscure factor and is best explained by a hypothetical situation. Let us take a match at a venue which holds a main head of fish in the 1lb class, the water is fast and powerful, probably running at around

2–3ft deep as is usual with this type of river. Without any hesitation, the choice of hook in this case would be the forged, crystal variety. And, conversely, if the water was of a more placid nature, say 6–10ft deep, and the species being sought was of a larger variety, probably in the 2lb plus bracket, because of the lack of assistance which the fish would receive from the current, the choice would be the fine-wire type.

Well, it can be argued, why not use a forged hook on all occasions, when surely the advantage in the strength of the hook can only be on the angler's side when a big fish is met up with. The answer to this is that the advantages of the fine-wire hook cannot be easily dismissed, and whenever possible they should be fully exploited. This is a hook ideally suited to the delicate caster because very little disfigurement is caused to the bait when it is mounted. And the same can be said for the maggot. Another big advantage of the fine-wire hook is its easy penetration of the fish. The tough texture of the fish's mouth is not always fully appreciated. This can easily be demonstrated by taking the head of a fish, say, a mackerel or a herring, and trying to set a hook in its mouth. This will bring full realization of exactly what is called for.

Unlike many other tackle items, hooks cannot be self-made at home but have to be purchased from the shops. The angler is therefore left with the job of amending them to suit his own personal requirements.

With the forged variety which we use, we consider it necessary to sharpen these using a fine carborundum stone, though this is not essential with the fine-wire pattern. The spade on the hook is also often very much out of proportion and, in its unadjusted form, can cause twisting and kinking of the line, especially when fishing longish swims in running water. This also has to be corrected with the carborundum stone, but care must be taken not to leave any sharp edges. We find it necessary to reduce the spade by as much as 50 per cent.

These adjustments to both point and spade result in the removal of the protective coat and this leaves the hook vulnerable to premature rusting. This can be easily prevented, however, by applying a smear of grease when both amending and tying the hook.

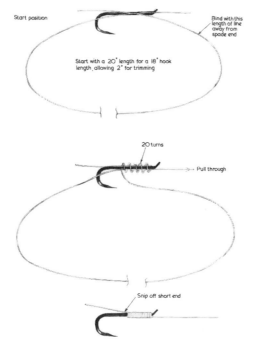

Start position

Bind with this length of line away from spade end

Start with a 20″ length for a 18″ hook length, allowing 2″ for trimming

20 turns

Pull through

Snip off short end

Fig 17 Hook tying

The hooks we use all have one thing in common—they do not have a barb. We believe this is absolutely essential if full and efficient penetration is to be achieved and, if the previously mentioned experiment is carried out, the angler will well realize that full advantage should be taken of every help in this direction. There are other advantages, too, not the least being the much easier removal of the hook from the fish, causing little or no damage. This also applies when the hook becomes snagged in items of clothing, such as sweaters, and in landing nets etc, where a barbed hook would become a scrap item.

Judging by the cross-section of match anglers we have rubbed shoulders with, top names among them, there are many shortcomings when it comes to tying hooks. Great experience is required to do this seemingly simple but vitally important job properly. The most common mistake seems to concern the number of loops made in whipping the hook. Far too many anglers consider that three, four, or perhaps five turns are ample. But we tend to think in terms of around twenty turns, which often extends the whipping to a position beyond the point of the hook if read on an imaginary horizontal line. Thorough whipping of this nature guarantees that the hook hangs perfectly, and cannot be easily offset by, say, the awkward unhooking of a fish, or any other form of mishandling. The recommended procedure for tying a hook is shown in Fig 17.

A tip here—do not tie a hook with a dry line. The procedure will be greatly facilitated either by passing the line between the lips to wet it, or, better still, by applying a smear of grease—in addition to assisting the tying procedure, this also removes any possibility of kinking.

It won't take long for the angler to familiarize himself with the varying hook sizes and breaking strains required to suit different conditions. But, this apart, hooks and lines must be kept in perspective. We see little use for, say, a size 20 hook for a $2\frac{1}{2}$–3lb line, or a great number of large hooks tied to a very fine breaking-strain line. A possible exception to this is the set-up for bread fishing when bream are sought.

Our hook formula is shown in the table below and we believe that a dozen and a half is the right number to carry in any particular size and breaking strain. If too many hooks and casts are made up, it can easily lead to quantities being left in the wallet of a large part of the season, with the possibility of deterioration.

Fine wire		Forged wire	
HOOK SIZE		HOOK SIZE	
24	to $\frac{3}{4}$ lb	18	to $1-1\frac{1}{2}$lb
22	to $\frac{3}{4}$ lb	16	to $1\frac{1}{2}-2\frac{1}{2}$lb
20	to $\frac{3}{4}-1$ lb	14	to $1\frac{1}{2}-2\frac{1}{2}-3\frac{1}{2}$lb
18	to $1-1\frac{1}{2}$ lb	12	to $2\frac{1}{2}-3\frac{1}{2}$lb
16	to $1-1\frac{1}{2}$ lb	10	to $2\frac{1}{2}-3\frac{1}{2}$lb
14	to $1\frac{1}{2}$ lb	8	tied direct
		6	tied direct

5 Lines and Shots

After discussing hooks, it is almost automatic that we turn to lines. And whilst most anglers are fully conscious of the importance of the hook, it is quite amazing how they tend to be careless and negligent when it comes to the line.

Let us first look at the properties required in a good line. There are so many on the market, some good, some bad, that the budding match angler will be well advised to seek a short cut in his final selection. This can very easily be done by carrying out a private survey among the better known matchmen. This will undoubtedly reveal that the majority all use a certain brand of line. Whilst this blind approach of following trends without knowing the reason behind them would not normally be advised, in this case it is, because, to get off the ground at all, a good line is essential.

The reason for the immense popularity of this one line is its all-round efficiency. Other products come through with flying colours on two or three salient points, only to fall short of the ideal in others. The factors to look for if this efficiency is to be obtained is the ability of a line to float; its resistance to kinking —a disadvantage which is accelerated by the retrieve when fishing moving water; a proportional diameter, and a practical colour.

Behind the hook, the line must rate as the most important item of tackle. Yet, while a large proportion of anglers are prepared to expend considerable sums of money on items of questionable use, they are content in many cases to fish a whole season with one line costing around 60p.

It may come as a surprise to many readers to learn that it is no rarity for us to fit a new line for a match and, after four hours of rainy conditions, either to scrap it completely or, at best, relegate it to a legering line.

Although in dry conditions a line can be used for match fishing up to about twenty hours and remain 100 per cent efficient as regards its floating properties, three or four hours' use in heavy rain completely destroys the ability to perform a clean strike, on which a floating line is so dependent.

From this it will be noted that we do not accept that a line to be used in conjunction with a float has a life of more than four contests. When considering the price, which is very favourable when compared to other tackle items, this penny-wise, pound-foolish attitude to lines leads to nothing but trouble.

Anglers are often misled into believing that a floating line is associated only with a float fished double rubber. This is not the case. In fact, if we had to come down on any one side, we would say that it was more important when used with a float fished from the bottom ring only. Admittedly, this applies to moving water, but let us for a moment deal with this type of fishing. When fishing bottom ring style, because of the float's independent nature, the least possible resistance should be met when mending the line. A line partially sinking will have the effect of pulling the float off course.

When legering, it is a distinct disadvantage to use a brand new line because of its float properties. An angler can, therefore, cut some of his losses by using his discarded lines for this purpose. It is generally accepted that a leger line does enjoy a longer life than one used for float fishing, and it is important that all lines should be kept out of direct sunlight when not in use.

There will be occasions when a fast-sinking line is necessary, or, in very shallow water, when the creating of an angle to assist sinking becomes an impossible task. In these instances, an application of liquid soap to the line will greatly assist in overcoming the difficulty. This can also apply to sinking lines used with heavy floats in windy Fenland conditions.

Very few lines are produced in this country. Most come from the Continent and are made with pole fishing in mind. These are often of a soft nature, and mainly white in colour. They are totally useless when used in moving water because the soft texture results in large-scale kinking. The harder types of lines, so ideally suited to our type of fishing, are invariably mist-grey in colour.

A line of 100 metres is ample for all normal match fishing requirements. When loading it on to the spool, which must be of a shallow pattern now common with all the best match reels, a simple slip-knot is all that is needed to secure it. When a close-face reel is being used, one should remember first to pass the line through the outer reel casing. The loading operation is best carried out by two people, one holding the spool square-face to the reel and applying finger pressure, the other person simply winding in the normal way at a consistent speed.

A good assortment of lines is recommended, and these should be on clearly marked spools. An ideal breakdown is as follows :

one $1\frac{1}{2}$lb line for use with a stick float and other double rubber varieties

one $1\frac{1}{2}$lb sinking line for use with canal darts, bleak tackle or light waggler fishing

one 2lb 6oz floating line for use in heavy-duty double rubber float fishing, or moving water waggler fishing

one $2\frac{1}{2}$lb wet line for use in legering, or for sunken line fishing in windy conditions

one 3lb line for barbel fishing, bread fishing and wasp grub fishing

one 3lb wet line for meat fishing

one very heavy line, around 8lb, for use when barbel fishing with a feeder

Though this is our shopping list for lines, slight adjustments will, of course, be necessary according to the areas being fished. For instance, in the Fenland angler's territory, floating lines are less common, so his list will allow for doubling up on the sinkers.

Increased commuting by anglers between this country and the Continent has led to considerable refinement of lead shots at the lower end of the scale. It seems only a short time since a No 8 shot, more popularly known as a 'dust', was considered the ultimate in fineness. But now we have at least four sizes smaller than this, though in all fairness their usefulness must be question-able in terms of English matchfishing styles. As far as the authors are concerned, the only use which lead shots are put to is to balance the tackle. Their employment as stops when legering is certainly not recommended.

There are somewhere around fourteen different sizes of shot available in the shops, but it is not necessary to carry the full range. A recommended selection is as follows : swan shot; treble A; BB; size 1; size 4; size 6; size 7; size 8; size 10, with the very occasional use of one of the miniature shots.

There are varying degrees of perfection in lead shots and it is advisable to select those with a high quality finish in terms of a central split and pure lead content, thus ensuring that they are of a consistently soft nature.

It is essential that lead shots are kept in a sealed container, free from dust or dirt, as it is important that the split remains clean in order to give a full grip on the line. The container chould be clearly marked with the various shot sizes.

Clive Smith comes under the camera

6 Miscellaneous Items

There are several miscellaneous items of tackle which, whilst perhaps not meriting detailed discussion, do warrant a mention.

First the *creel*. Several materials have been tried in the manufacture of the fisherman's basket—glass-fibre, aluminium, PVC, and so on. But it is our very firm opinion that there is nothing to replace the wicker basket. This has been emphasized more than ever by the amendment of NFA match rules to allow standing in the river margins during a match.

After being emptied of its contents, the wicker basket can be positioned in the river to serve as a first-class table top. With other materials, such a use has obvious disadvantages—either they do not take to being immersed in water or, in the case of materials such as fibre-glass, they tend to float.

An item which has received increased attention over the past few years is the *rod bag*. There have been many new designs brought onto the market, zip-ups, roll-up types, and so on, but for practicability and efficiency there is nothing to match the sling type. Generously designed to carry five $2\frac{1}{2}$in diameter lightweight protective rod tubes, there is also room for other tackle items.

It rules out the necessity of tight strapping of bank sticks and similar items against thin-walled fibre-glass rods, thus causing bruising which so often results in eventual breakage. The individual packing of rods is also a big advantage, it eliminates possible ring damage by rods being forced down upon each other.

Keep-nets are now sensibly governed by River Authority bylaws, but anglers would be well advised to go in for the larger sizes. This does assist in the preservation of fish and is in the long-term interests of the sport. An ideal length is 10–12ft, with supporting rings not less than 18in diameter and a top aperture ring of 24in diameter. This offers distinct advantages when bleak fishing.

The smooth type micromesh net which has been developed during the last few years is ideal, especially when barbel are to be contained. This can also be vital in major matches, such as the National Championships, for containing one single fish. Periodical checks should be made for signs of wear or damage to the net, and the retaining ring at the bottom should be given particularly close scrutiny.

For the *landing net* a larger mesh is recommended as this offers assistance in quick displacement of water on netting a fish. A mesh diameter about twice that of micromesh is quite suitable. This safeguards against the possibility of leger weights finding their way through the net, thus causing unnecessary time-wasting when fish are on the feed.

The landing net should have as large a ring as possible; 24in is ideal for normal match fishing. The depth should not be too great, around 14–16in, and it should be of the pan variety. An 8ft pole is ideal, either telescopic or two-jointed, and made either of glass or light alloy. The thread should be carefully checked.

Waders have now become more or less an essential item with the amending of NFA wading rules, plus the annual increase in boat traffic. There are added advantages of wearing waders which will soon become obvious, protection against early-season, long grass being just one.

When *catapults* were made eligible in major contests, first designs were the solid-cup types, and these were quickly followed by many other varieties. The discomfort of this solid-cup catapult when bouncing back was quickly realized by anglers, and the most popular type currently is that made of smooth, supple leather. The main thing to remember about the catapult—always carry a spare!

Turning to *disgorgers*, there are four or five different varieties on the market but the match angler would be well advised to concentrate on the tube type. It is the easiest to use and does not damage the line. However, it should be remembered that, being made of aluminium, it does not float and it is advisable always to carry at least two or three at a contest.

Rod rests and *bank sticks.* There are two types of rod-rest heads, the large size used for float fishing, and the smaller leger patterns. The former should have a minimum bridge of 7in, made of tubular rubber or plastic to minimize line damage. For the leger type, the bridge is no more than 3in and an important feature is the clearance slot situated at the base of the 'V', vital when 'twitching' or setting a swing- or quiver-tip. This is best used in conjunction with a two-part adjustable bank stick as the swing-tip or quiver-tip has to be set at a critical height to the water and it is so much easier to adjust the wing nut than to either push or pull a bank stick.

A bank stick around 4ft long is ideal for float fishing, though a greater length is needed for swimfeeder fishing to allow the rod to be positioned nearly vertical. This will obviously be of the telescopic variety. Other bank sticks are for keep-nets, and all threads should be interchangeable, ⅜in BSF.

An *apron* is a vital item of tackle and far superior to the clumsy bait stands and trays placed round the angler which only create an obstacle course for the incoming fish. With the apron attached to the body, it is automatically found by the hand in any position, whereas with bait receptacles situated independent of the angler, these have to be observed each time bait is needed. A smooth vinyl or PVC material is recommended for the apron.

On rivers prone to flooding, a *spade* is invaluable for creating a comfortable position. A *scythe* used in conjunction with a landing-net pole is also most useful at the start of the season when there is an abundance of pandocks and other bankside vegetation.

A clean, dry, standard-type *towel* should always be carried.

A *sun visor* is essential and equally important in winter and summer.

A small container of *grease* should be carried. It is most useful on stormy days to counteract premature sinking of the reel line.

A small airtight tin containing a sponge immersed in liquid *soap* can be very useful when legering, especially in shallow water, when the sinking of the line can be difficult.

A length of $\frac{1}{8}$in diameter silicone rubber will provide the angler with all the *float caps* he requires.

Where possible, *bait boxes* should be of metal. They far out-last the plastic types which are susceptible to breakage, especially in cold weather. A large airtight plastic container should be kept aside for casters.

A groundbait *bowl* is necessary. It should be as large as possible to fit neatly into the creel, with rounded corners and of a smooth finish.

At least one *carrying bag* is required for the nets which are best kept separate from the creel as a lot of water drains from them after a contest. The bag materials should be rot-proof and the bag designed so that it remains clear of the ground when carried.

Only in exceptional circumstances do we recommend the use of an *umbrella* and this can be narrowed down to wet winter days when pursuing a static form of fishing, and when the backs of the hands are subjected to sleet and snow.

A good *waterproof coat* is important, essentially incorporating a fixed hood. For anglers who do not, in the main, use brollies, this coat will stand between them and a good soaking. A three-quarter-length coat is ideal, with separate *waterproof trousers*. The 'all-in-ones' are not for us, mainly because they don't lend themselves to easy removal in changeable weather conditions when an adjustment of clothing is essential.

Stemming from the revision of NFA match rules in 1970, the *swimfeeder* has now found a place in the baskets of all serious matchmen. Justifiably so, too, because the effectiveness, of what at first sight may seem to be a cumbersome and crude item of tackle, can only be judged by the consistent results it produces throughout the season. Its effectiveness is not restricted to either big-weight or small-weight contests. It is equally successful at all levels. It very often contributes to the best weight recorded in a season, and can also be a sound method for catching that odd fish in unfavourable winter conditions.

There are several types of feeders on the market, and they tend to follow two patterns, the block-end and open-end varieties. The open end needs groundbait to retain the feed in the

56

cylinder, but the block end can be used for neat bait, if required.

By far the largest size range comes in the block-end type, spanning from models holding a good handful of neat maggots and measuring $1\frac{1}{2}$in x $2\frac{3}{4}$in, commonly used for catching barbel in summer and autumn, to the small varieties often associated with winter fishing when smaller amounts of feed are consumed.

Another aid legalized by the rules change is the *bait dropper*. Although this does not enjoy the same popularity as the feeder, it has its uses which tend to be exploited more in the southern part of the country where the widespread nuisance of surface-feeding bleak creates a definite use for such a bait depositor.

Another use for the bait dropper is on fast-flowing waters, especially where barbel are resident and the feed bait is most effective on the riverbed.

7 Baits

Most baits are easy to obtain these days, and the choice can vary considerably depending upon the type of water to be fished, the time of year, conditions on the day, and so on. Some types of bait mean big fish, while others are for the smaller varieties, and there is still something of an air of mystery about some baits, principally in areas where they are rarely, if ever, used. One instance of this is the *bloodworm*.

One bait which is not readily obtainable is the *wasp grub*. Properly used in the right conditions, this can be deadly for chub and some anglers go to great lengths to obtain it. But, for one reason or another, the wasp grub is banned in many contests, and we don't intend to take sides on this issue.

From all this the reader will gather that many factors are involved in the selection of the right bait for a particular match. This is determined only by experience.

The most popular of modern baits and one which, for consistency, must take the crown, is the *caster*. This bait must account for more fish than all others put together and it makes the mind boggle just to think of the quantities which must be used throughout the country on just one weekend of the busy matchfishing season. It is a bait which must be looked at in some detail.

In our opinion it is not really worthwhile for an angler to turn his own casters. This view stems from experience in the commercial production of the bait and knowledge of the quantities of maggots which must be set aside in proportion to the amount of casters required. Even with a good yield, the ratio is usually

Ken Giles with the catch, mainly of bream, which won him the South West Regional Embassy Semi-final on the Bristol Avon

no more than a pint of casters from a gallon of maggots, on a given day. Assuming that four pints of fresh casters are needed for a Sunday match, this would involve turning four gallons of maggots. One could be fortunate in obtaining a 50 per cent 'turn' in one day, but obviously, this cannot be left to chance as there is little use in discovering too late that insufficient maggots have been put down. And Saturday night is not the best time to go seeking an extra couple of pints of casters!

The angler who is most likely to try and produce his own bait is the keener type of matchman. But it is going to work against him, because, to obtain the right amount, he will have to store them over a period of two or three days, and by then they have lost their freshness. It is a much better policy to select a tackle shop well known for supplying good quality bait.

An important point about the caster is its colour. It is a mistake to have them all the same colour because this means that the density is the same and they will all fall through the water at the same level. It is essential to obtain a staggered fall of feed through the water so that the caster with the added weight of the hook does not stand out, but is disguised among the loose bait thrown in. It follows from this that a white, or straw-coloured, caster, containing 100 per cent liquid and no air, will make the fastest drop. The best hook caster, which will align itself with the fall, is therefore one of this colour, or one in the first stage of its change from a maggot. This is even more important if the fish are being caught 'on the drop'.

Great attention should be paid to attaching the caster to the hook. Only occasionally should the hook be completely buried, invariably on canals and lakes, or when bites are going to be few and far between. Apart from this, the best method is to hook the caster in a similar way to a maggot, possibly a little deeper.

When fishing two casters at long distance, hook spin may occur. To avoid this a good tip is to attach one caster in the normal manner, with the other only lightly hooked through the pointed end. On the strike at the end of the swim down, this second caster will remove itself from the hook and line spin will be avoided. Where possible we favour a barbless fine-wire hook which gives clean penetration and eliminates the white blob which is customary when the barbed variety is used.

It must be remembered that a caster is a living creature and there is a limit to the length of time it can be kept. The life cycle can be retarded by storage in a refrigerator, but it cannot be stopped altogether, and a three-day period seems to be the maximum to retain a caster suitable for use.

In warm days by the riverside, a supply of casters will not remain usable even for the duration of a match, if left in the sun. Storage in a properly sealed container, in the shade, is the best way. It also pays to carry them in small pots, taped, for use pint by pint, rather than to take the bulk in one large container. Deterioration is less of a problem during the winter months, although attention must till be given to keeping them fresh and crisp.

The *maggot* has for long been a very popular bait among anglers, and is obtainable in many varieties. The commercial maggot in itself is frowned upon by some but it must be said that, with certain types of fishing, this bait has a distinct advantage. For instance, when bleak and dace fishing, several fish can be caught without having to change the bait, and, in a contest, this time-saving is invaluable. This cannot be done with a more specialized maggot with a softer skin. The commercial maggot can be purchased ready for use, over the counter, and, for the angler who is colour-conscious, they are obtainable in four or five different colours in most areas of the country. It is a simple bait, but still very usable.

The more sophisticated type of maggot, the aristocrat, is the *gozzer*. For several reasons this will catch fish when other varieties fail. And strange as it may seem, confidence plays a big part in this. There is something about putting a gozzer on the hook and expecting that little extra response from the fish.

The main definition of the gozzer is its softness compared with the ordinary maggot. It can be bred to varying sizes, depending upon when it is taken off the feed, and at all times it must be kept damp in a non-abrasive substance. Moist bran is ideal, although it should be pointed out that this is susceptible to 'going off' rather quickly, especially in warm weather. Perhaps best known for its success with bream, even at four or five days old, the gozzer will still be softer than an ordinary fresh maggot.

After experimenting with many forms of meat, we have found pigeon to be superior for producing the ideal gozzer. For one thing, the feathers prevent the meat from becoming dry. Preferably, the bird should be situated well away from housefly attractions, such as dustbins and other rubbish, say, a position at the top of a garden. And it is no use putting out a complete pigeon because a mass of blow can be hidden by the feathers. It is best to remove the head of the bird and put this out to obtain the 'blow' which can be seen much more easily. At the blown stage, the head should then be placed in the body of the bird after an incision has been made, and put into a container with a muslin top, to keep out other flies. A quantity of bran should be put into the container to absorb any condensation, and it should be kept in a dark, cool position—the best gozzers are produced in a refrigerator set around 38°F (3·3°C).

When not refrigerated, the period of time from the blow to production of a full size gozzer in the summer months is nine days. It may be, of course, that the maximum size is not required and, in this case, the growth has to be intercepted at the required stage. The full-size gozzer will fall off the bird on its own, smaller samples should be shaken off, and always stored in damp bran.

If colouring is needed, this should be applied to the meat, and not to the gozzers after production. However, we tend to believe that the natural colour is best. It is a delicate maggot, easily penetrable, and recommended for use with a fine-wire hook.

Another maggot variety is the *pinkie*. This is the larvae of the greenbottle and is often used as a replacement for the gozzer during the winter months. Care is needed in storing this bait, as it has the ability to walk up most vertical surfaces. It is readily available commercially and is ideal for catching fish in the 2–6oz class, and also as feed for the more static type of waters.

The pinkie is often used as a feeder bait in conjunction with a larger maggot, or a gozzer, on the hook, and can be kept in a refrigerator for longer periods than other types of maggots. When used as a hookbait, a fine-wire design of hook is recommended.

The *squatt* is the larvae of the housefly and plays a supporting role to more sophisticated hookbaits. It is a popular feeding bait among bream anglers and also on the canals, and has the ability to break up groundbait when used in still water. It is readily obtainable during the summer months, but can become scarce in certain areas of the country during the winter. Unlike other maggots, squatts are kept in sand rather than cereal compounds. It is a delicate bait to store and is averse to low temperatures. It cannot stand long periods of refrigeration in the same way as other maggots and should be taken out of cold storage on alternate days.

There are occasions when the squatt can be promoted to a hookbait. When fish are extremely hard to tempt, a few squatts on a size 20 hook will often bring success. More commonly, it is used as a canal hookbait for gudgeon and small roach.

Bread can be a highly successful bait and, when used on the hook, usually takes two forms—bread punch and flake. The punch is mainly used on still water, such as canal fishing, although in the western areas of the country it is commonly used in river fishing for larger sample fish.

When punch fishing, a medium slice of close-grain bread from a new loaf should be used. This is best kept in a polythene bag or container. Bread-flake, used for larger fish, mainly bream and chub, should also be taken from a new loaf. Methods of fishing with bread are dealt with in a later chapter.

Seed baits—hemp, tares and wheat—are all noted as being seasonal baits, closely associated with roach. They are used with most success from about harvest time until the first frosts signal the end of their reign. Correct preparation is the key to these baits as they are totally unusable on purchase and resemble gravel or grit. The seeds have to be softened by boiling and, although experience will quickly determine when the baits are ready for use, this can be judged, especially with wheat and tares, by the feel of the seeds. If they can be compressed by the fingers, then they are usable. With hemp it is much easier, as the white seed penetrating from the shell signals its readiness.

These baits can be kept in any sort of container but in warm weather they are liable to go rancid very quickly, and in this condition their introduction to a swim is not advisable. For convenience, there is no reason why a number of packs of seed baits should not be prepared and placed in a deep-freeze for later use. Some anglers add bicarbonate of soda during the boiling process and, although we have tried this, we have not found it to be particularly advantageous.

The *worm* is another well used bait and, among match anglers, the red worm is by far the most popular. The lobworm is mainly the province of the specimen hunter. It is in the winter months when the red worm comes into its own around the bream-fishing strongholds and is very often a substitute for the summer gozzer. It can be obtained from tackle shops, but many anglers have a corner in the garden where a few red worms can be obtained at short notice. They are very easy to store and will last for months in an ordinary bait box providing it is well ventilated and kept free from frost.

Bloodworms and *jokers* are a more complex bait. They are found under water and are becoming more easily obtainable from tackle shops. They are extremely difficult to keep for any length of time, especially the joker, which is the feed to the bloodworm hookbait in a similar manner to the squatt and the gozzer. Large quantities are needed to fish a match, and some anglers use up to three pints of neat jokers to catch a weight of around 3lb of fish. Peat seems to be the only substance which these worms find acceptable in their unnatural surroundings, out of water.

Through our travels in the Continent we observed that the French and Belgian anglers prefer a variety of damp, chopped leaves for storage, and then, prior to a match, they transfer the baits to sphagnum moss which, they assure us, puts a shine on the bait! On both ides of the Channel, however, damp newspaper folded into squares seems the ideal container. These can be placed in a refrigerator to prolong the life of the worms, at a temperature of around 38°F (3·3°C).

8 Groundbait

Groundbait is like dynamite, it should always be treated with the greatest respect. It can make or break a swim, and an angler can never afford to be the least bit careless in its use.

The principle of groundbaiting is, most often, to get a quantity of the bait which is being used on the hook laid in the area where it is hoped to catch fish. It follows, then, that the farther the distance from the bank an angler is fishing, the more important the role which groundbait has to play.

The definition of groundbait can take two forms. It can be interpreted as the loose-fed hookbait which baits the fishing ground, or as a substance which carries the bait out to the fishing point. On the very odd occasion, cereal groundbait can be used on its own as a fish attractor, most notably in conjunction with a bread punch. All that needs to be added are a few larger particles of bread to simulate the sample on the hook.

In some areas of the country, such as the Fens, anglers grow up with groundbait and are fully accomplished in its use. Yet in other parts, and we must admit that these do include our 'home' territory in the Midlands, groundbaiting is something of a lost art. Even some of our best matchmen have had glittering careers with very little use of groundbait, and this can probably be put down to a predominance in the area of chub, a fish which is not particularly linked with heavy groundbaiting, mostly preferring loose feed.

It is easy to go wrong with groundbait for the simple reason that a bad mix can never be put right. The first requirement is a plastic mixing bowl, 5–6in deep, with as large a surface area as possible, which will fit into the creel or carrier. It is important that the bowl has rounded corners as this not only makes mixing easier, it eliminates the possibility of dry, unmixed bait being left in the corners.

Groundbait is added to water and *not* vice versa. This is important. It is not easy to mix, and ensuring that the dry bait has to travel through the water helps to rule out the possibility of some of it remaining dry among the mix.

It will help the novice considerably if he realizes that there is no short cut to the proper mixing of groundbait. Although it looks easy, it can be difficult to get right. It must be given a lot of attention, and then proficiency will come with practice and experience. The consistency of groundbait varies considerably according to the conditions under which it is being used. First of all there is the stiff variety, the easiest of all to mix, which requires nothing more than plain ground white bread, the normal white groundbait, obtainable from the tackle shop, which should be as near as possible 100 per cent bread.

For moving water, such as on the Severn, Hampshire Avon and Norfolk Broads, what we term the 'heavy' rivers, a grain slightly smaller than a pinhead is required. The groundbait obviously has to be of a stout variety because, although, ideally, in other instances it should break on impact with the water, this is an exceptional case.

The reason for this is fairly obvious. Let us take a typical swim on this 'heavy' type of river. The depth can be anything up to 16ft, the current can be powerful, if not necessarily fast. And the aim is to deposit the groundbait on the bed of the river— before it starts breaking up. If it were to disintegrate on surface impact, as in other instances, the bait would be distributed over an area far too vast to have any practical use.

For this type of river, in fact, the groundbait can never be too stiff. If reassurance is needed that the mix will break up on the riverbed, and within a reasonably short time, a simple experiment can be carried out.

Take a sample ball of groundbait from the bowl and place it in a few inches of water at the side of the river. Even without any effect from the current, the ball will flatten in a matter of minutes. And the more bait, such as maggots and casters, it contains, so will the break-up be accelerated.

A good tip when using groundbait of this type is to glaze the ball before throwing it in. The angler will require a handily placed utensil half filled with water unless, of course, he is conveniently placed so as to be able to dip his hands in the river. It is important to follow this procedure—first dip both hands in the water and shake off the surplus, then mould the ball to the required size, adding the feeders or maggots as necessary. When the ball has been fashioned, dip the hands in the water again and rotate the ball of groundbait so as to cover its surface with water from the hands.

This glazing reduces the friction on impact and ensures that the ball enters the water all in one piece. The noise is also much less when the groundbait is treated in this way and, as a bonus advantage, it also cleans the hands.

In all forms of groundbaiting it is always advisable to select a marker on the far bank as a precautionary measure. The bait may be thrown in at varying periods during a match, and there may be long lulls between baiting. It is very easy to forget the exact location in the swim where the bait was introduced, and this is where a marker can be extremely useful.

Although specific methods of catching fish are dealt with in a later chapter, it is perhaps opportune to mention here that, when introducing feeder baits into the swim with groundbait, for example, maggots, squatts, pinkies, etc, these must be added to each ball of groundbait and not to the whole bowlful of mix. Casters are an exception.

The right method is to place the grubs on top of the groundbait, and then gather the ball around them. The mistake is so often made whereby a complete mix of groundbait is made and to this is added the full quota of maggots or other bait thought to be needed for the match. This can lead to a position where the angler is finally left with something like a pint of maggots and two pints of groundbait in the bowl.

Groundbait should always be made up in small quantities at a time, one reason being that chemical reaction takes place and the mix can change over a period of five hours. This is accentuated in warmer weather. Ideally, no more than an hour's supply should be mixed at a time.

As a general guide to the type and consistency of groundbait required for varying waters, as the pace of a river becomes slower, the less stiff the mixture is required to be. The correct consistency is acquired by adding brown groundbait to the white variety, previously mentioned, in varying degrees. For a moderate flow it therefore follows that the mix will comprise about equal proportions of white and brown groundbait, whilst on still water it will be purely brown.

These mixes must be carried out dry, and very thoroughly. The consistency will be looser than the pure white type, and, ideally, it will be required to break up somewhere around a third of the way down the depth of the swim. An experienced angler knows when his mix is right by the noise it makes on entering the water.

With a stiff groundbait, a quantity about cricket-ball size is needed to cope with the current, but, with a more moderate flowing water, an amount which can be taken from the bowl with one hand, with the fingers clasped around it, is sufficient. It is even more important, with this groundbait texture, to wet the hand first, as it tends to break up much more easily and cling to the hand, if dry. Here again, feed baits should be added only as needed.

Mixing groundbait for still waters is the biggest challenge. This is usually 100 per cent brown, although a little white can be added if it is to be used at exceptional distances, or against strong facing winds where breaking in flight is being experienced.

This tends to be used on the larger expanses of water such as the wide-ranging rivers of the Fens, or various lakes up and down the country. Achieving efficiency at this type of ground-baiting is not easy and a great deal of practice is needed before a satisfactory standard is obtained. Whilst accepting the fact that still waters offer the greatest challenge when dealing with the subject of groundbait, this becomes even more severe in shallow water. One typical venue which comes to mind is Coombe Abbey Lake, near Coventry, a nationally known water where the depth rarely exceeds 4ft.

Here the resident match-winning species is invariably bream and no doubt this venue resembles many others up and down the country. In situations of this kind the match angler can gain great advantage by using casters in his groundbait.

Unlike 'active' baits, such as maggots, squatts or pinkies, the caster lies dormant on the riverbed until found by the shoals of fish searching for feed. This, then, does away with the necessity of frequent feeding and in the shallow conditions, and eliminates much of the disturbance to the swim which this feeding causes, which can be a factor of vital importance.

When introducing casters into the groundbait, it is very effective if two-thirds of them are crushed. In our interpretation this creates a similar situation to the human liking for meat. Whilst a steak does not immediately sharpen the appetite when on the butcher's slab, when the juices have been disturbed by the chef in cooking, it immediately becomes much more appetizing. It is the same with the crushed caster.

The success of this manoeuvre was clearly shown at Coombe Abbey Lake during a hard fought Ladbroke Super League match. Ken introduced his groundbait-caster combination for the very reasons which have just been explained. He did not have the fortune to be drawn in an area containing bream but with the use of this type of baiting, he was able to fish with confidence in the knowledge that without further disturbance to his swim, he had sufficient feed out there to attract passing fish.

With only 45 minutes of the match left, and a dry net seeming to be very much on the cards—a disaster in this type of points-deciding event—his swing-tip lifted and a four-pound bream was on the way to the net!

This was repeated another four times before the end of the match and Ken weighed in seventeen pounds of fish to finish second in his section.

It is well worth while devoting some time to visiting a waterside with nothing more than a supply of groundbait and a bowl. It may look silly to a passer-by, but to obtain mastery of this groundbaiting technique gives an angler tremendous confidence, and this can be invaluable at a big match. There is nothing worse than fishing in front of a gallery of spectators and 'drying up' in confidence when a ball of groundbait has to be thrown, say thirty or forty yards, and the angler is not capable of doing it. To master the technique, there is no substitute for practice.

For canal fishing there are various groundbaits. Firstly there is the type used in conjunction with a bread punch, the 'odd man out' among groundbaits in that it is the only one which does not carry maggots or casters. It is a very fine mix, either brown or white, and this is achieved with the use of the finest sieve available. It should really be of a similar texture to flour, and to it can be added large crumbs in the ratio of one table-spoonful per pint of fine groundbait.

The crumbs are, of course, the substitute for the maggots and casters in other forms of groundbait, and simulate the hookbait. The mix should be on the dry side, so that it just holds together. In this way, particles will sink as they absorb water through the swim, long after the original entry of the groundbait into the water.

On windy days, when there is considerable surface movement, care should be taken to ensure that the groundbait does not drift out of the swim and become deposited over a wide area. The way round this problem is to make a wetter mix. A pint should be ample for any canal match.

Another groundbait commonly used on canals is the one for carrying squatts or pinkies, invariably when fishing for either bream or gudgeon. This is also of a very fine consistency but, unlike the bread-punch bait, is of a wet nature, strong enough to be thrown through the air before breaking up. It can best be described as a 'sloppy' mix, of a very fine nature, and should be fed into the swim on the 'little and often' principle because one of the main advantages of this bait lies in its clouding capacity. For this groundbait, too, the quantity needed for a normal match would be somewhere around a pint, and it is advisable to use a receptable smaller than that employed in river fishing. If the bowl is too large, the mix tends to dry out during the contest. For this purpose, in fact, a 2-pint maggot pot is ideal. A groundbait similar to that just described will be ideal for small roach up to the 2–3oz range. For fish above this we tend to favour loose-fed caster or maggot.

There is one groundbait which has a different function from the others; that used in conjunction with bloodworms. It has to have properties which allow it to deposit the jokers on the bed of the canal. If introduced independently, by the loose-feed method, for example, the jokers will float because of their greasy coating, acquired since their removal from their natural environment.

Clive Smith in action netting a fish at a local reservoir

They will then just drift away, having served no useful purpose.

When the jokers are deposited firmly on the canal bed, the greasy coating becomes neutralized and, in a short period of time, they assume their natural activity of remaining well down in water, propelling themselves with a jerky movement and, in the process, lifting themselves anything up to an inch off the canal bed.

The type of groundbait used to perform this function is a mixture of peat, brown bread, and mole hills, in the ratio of two-thirds mole hill and the other third equally divided between the peat and brown bread. The mole hills should be collected as dry as possible to obtain the finest texture, and should be sieved through a groundbait riddle, together with the peat. They should then be mixed with the brown groundbait prior to use. If mixed too soon it will be found that the damp molehills will sour the bread. Contrary to all the principles of groundbaiting in still water, this mix is used in very solid form, resembling the stiff variety previously described for strong-flowing rivers, possibly even heavier. It never ceases to amaze us how quickly the fish return to this addictive bait after its somewhat disruptive introduction in depths of only 3–4ft.

In this chapter we have kept strictly to the ingredients and mixes of the various groundbaits. Later in the book we will deal specifically with the varying species and the right groundbaiting approach associated with them.

PART TWO

Methods and Tactics

9 Bream

If an angler had to select one fish around which match fishing has principally revolved over the past decade, he would surely go for bream. This was, of course, before the days of the big barbel and chub catches in the Severn. Bream were always the heavyweight contenders on the match scene, and all the sensationalism used to be centred around them. This applied to the nationals in which the bream rivers were given all the attention. The most successful method of catching bream used to be with a float. This was in the days of Coventry's ascendancy in the '60s when heavy antenna designs, used in conjunction with plenty of groundbait, outstripped other methods. But then came the development of leger tactics by certain Fenland anglers and this was undoubtedly a contributing factor to the relaxing of the Coventry stranglehold.

The advantages of the leger were enormous. It was a counter to the persistent high winds in the low-lying Fen district, and proved a much more efficient method of compiling a big weight than the float, which could be relied upon to attain satisfactory bait presentation only in perfect conditions.

Though the Fens are perhaps the best known area for bream, the species can be found in many other parts of the country, such as the West Midlands, Norfolk Broads, West Country, and so on. And they can be approached either with float or leger with the different venues in mind. Although generally considered to be a still- or slow-moving water species, they are often found in large numbers in faster flowing rivers such as the Broads and some Severn venues.

Though the general approach is the same in either case, important alterations have to be made to tackle and feeding patterns if success is to be achieved on varying waters. Let us first take a look at the approach to the match on a Fenland-type water, such as the Welland or Witham, or lakes such as Coombe Abbey, near Coventry, which have gained recognition as top bream venues.

As a first priority, the competitor must be realistic and accept as fact that if any measure of success is to be achieved, it is imperative to be drawn in an area which is noted for bream. These localities are well known on all the top match venues. This has been assisted by permanent pegging and, of course, the publishing of results in the angling Press each week. Bream are very predictable in terms of movement. They rarely, if ever, stray into the 'barren' areas, a fact well known to those anglers who fish the bream rivers week after week.

During the last few years of crowded match calendars the shoals of bream in the various waters have been monitored almost weekly. But, a few years ago, when these fish concentrations were not so apparent, large amounts of groundbait were thought to be the answer to drawing and settling the fish into a swim. As has since been proved, this was an abortive measure, and could well have proved disastrous in the case where the bream were already there in the swim prior to the groundbait bombardment.

Based on this realization that the whereabouts of the bream are known, a competitor is now able to concentrate on catching them without having to think about luring them into the area. And the main point emerging from this surrounds the quantity of feed needed to fish a five-hour match. Instead of the old practice when anglers would carry, and very often use, 20lb of groundbait plus a gallon of squatts and other baits, the approach is now made very successfully with 4 or 5lb of groundbait of a much lighter consistency, and probably a half-gallon of squatts, or even casters.

In the case of a match being fished along only one bank of the river, with few exceptions the bream become resident along the far margin, or at a distance of about 35–40yds out in the case of a pool or lake.

On a majority of occasions it will be found that leger tackle is the ideal tool for bream. One common mistake here, though, is to employ a weight which is far too light. In terms of fishing at a distance of 30yd or more, a $\frac{3}{4}$oz bomb is certainly not too heavy. To go any lighter than this will tend to lead to the line governing the leger in the initial settling phase rather than achieve an ideal anchoring manoeuvre with the heavier design. As with a float, 2$\frac{1}{2}$lb line is perfect, but it must be a good sinker.

The only leger set-up we use is the paternoster style with a lead link of 6–8in and a tail varying between 4–6ft, the longer measure being implemented in a situation where the bream are inclined to feed on the drop.

As mentioned in a previous chapter, we always work on preparing bait to last for sixty or ninety minutes only. If casters are being used—and, incidentally, they are an exceptionally good bream bait—then the desired quantity can be mixed in the initial stage. But if squatts are chosen, then a pinch of these should be added to each ball of groundbait as and when required. If these were introduced into the mix initially, they would all work to the bottom of the bowl.

At the start of a match, an exploratory cast with either of the selected methods should be made, to ensure that the swim has a clear, snag-free bottom. Then four balls of groundbait, about egg-size and mixed as lightly as possible consistent with ensuring that they reach the required area without breaking up, should be thrown in at a selected position past mid-river. It is not desirable to introduce the balls all at the same spot, but human error is usually a sufficient factor to prevent this, and give an ideal feeding pattern. For finer details, it is perhaps worth referring back to the chapter dealing with groundbaiting.

This initial groundbaiting will be sufficient to retain any bream in the swim during the early stages of the match, but further groundbaiting at this stage could be very harmful. It is essential that the fish are allowed to gain confidence, and it could well take them twenty minutes to become preoccupied with the feed.

Though it is always nice to get a good start to a match, we believe that it is not a good sign to catch bream too early. The feeding pattern and confidence of the fish can be gauged by the quantity of fish being taken. For example, a good start to a match would be to take a brace, say, in the second half-hour.

This would give encouragement to add one ball of groundbait every fifteen minutes. If the river was flat calm, more care would have to be taken and very often indicates the use of a catapult, with smaller balls of groundbait, on the little and often principle.

If the fish keep coming, there is no need to diverge from this pattern. But the problem arises when they cease feeding. Very often at this type of venue, good vision of other competitors in the near vicinity is available, and judgement as to future tactics can be guided by how they are faring. If it is apparent that no fish are being caught in the area, then it would not be politic to carry out further groundbaiting. It would obviously be a simple case of the fish going off the feed, and more bait would certainly not be the answer. In a situation like this it is just a case of sitting it out and waiting for the bream to start feeding again.

If, however, it is apparent that a competitor nearby is consistently taking fish, then this calls for a different approach. It would indicate that the bream *are* in a feeding mood, but the angler concerned is not getting his fair share. It could be that insufficient feed had been introduced, and a calculated gamble must be taken to try and regenerate the swim. This could take the form of another four balls of groundbait similar to those introduced at the start, and if this brought results then it would be a clear indication that a slight increase in feed was the answer. This feeding pattern would apply in the case of either float or leger fishing.

Another important factor surrounds the hook-size best suited to bream fishing at the popular match venues. For the most common bait, the gozzer, an 18 or 20 of the forged variety, is recommended, tied to a 1lb bottom. If the fish were really going well, perhaps a 1½lb cast could be substituted, but there is little reason to go larger than an 18 hook.

If conditions are perfect, then a float can be considered. But it must be realized that a bait intended for bream may have to be in the water for some considerable time. These fish aren't caught every two or three minutes, so it seems that, when deciding on his approach, a competitor has to weigh up whether he can present a bait successfully by means of a float for the length of time it may be needed to catch a bream. And this means taking into account wind velocity and current.

Float fishing is the ideal method of enticing bream to feed. It can present a much more natural movement of the bait than the static nature of a leger presentation. As most bream fishing is done at a distance, however, the float must be of a substantial shotting capacity, something in the region of 4 swans. Also, it is a fact that the lowland regions of this country produce the slow-moving water in which large quantities of bream reside. Unfortunately, because of their flat nature, these regions also suffer from troublesome wind conditions, thus necessitating the sinking of the line between the float and the rod tip. By far the best type of float is one which incorporates the body at the base end.

Finally, on this type of water there will invariably be surface movement, caused by waves, and this demands a float of con-

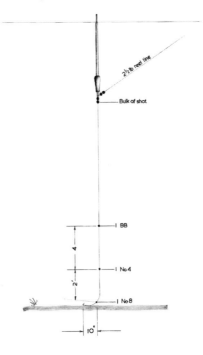

Fig 18 The total amount of shot should be such that it allows the angler to cast 5yd past the area required with ease

siderable length. Often it will average in the region of 14in, even under ideal conditions.

Because of the shotting capacity, a 2½lb line is essential. The float is set some 6in over depth, and shotted as shown in Fig 18. A size 20 forged hook can be used in most cases, but where the fish run to 2–3lb a step up to an 18 would be advised.

Casting should be made to a point well past the area to be fished, about five yards in fact, so that the complete line from rod tip to float—and this can be 30yd plus—can be sunk out of harm's way. Drawing back the line to the area to be fished gives a straight line between the hook and the float, thus making it much easier for a bite to be read on the thin antenna should a bream intercept the bait on its way down to the riverbed.

If excessive depths are encountered, making it difficult to fish a fixed float, then the sliding version should be selected. The above format should be observed. The only variation would be in the shotting pattern and this was fully described in the chapter on floats, while Fig 15 detailed the shotting arrangement. Feeding patterns, hook selection, etc, are exactly the same as those for legering.

For worm bait, which comes into its own from autumn onwards, a 16 forged hook would be the choice with a 1½lb hooklength. This is because the worm tends to attract the larger fish and also, for some reason, autumn and winter bream do tend to fight that little bit harder.

With bread fishing, a bait most likely to produce results very early in the season, the hook would be a size 10 or 12, but not necessarily of the forged type. There are some very good fine-wire designs on the market and, when talking in terms of larger sizes of hook, the strength is more than sufficient at this size, with the added advantage of having a better class point.

The mistake is often made, when using larger hooks, of employing heavy breaking-strain lines. We consider that 1½lb is ideal, its selection being for the same reason as for worm fishing, that bread does tend to attract the larger fish.

Bream are generally connected with slow-moving, placid waters, but there are also vast shoals resident in some of our strong-running rivers, such as the Severn, or tidal reaches of the Norfolk system, which perhaps, theoretically, ought to be suitable for the more robust chub or barbel. Because of the different environment in which these bream exist, there has to be a marked difference in some of the tactics employed in catching them. In fact, probably the only similarity between the Fenland bream and the strong-water inhabitants is that they are both sought on the riverbed.

In strong-water conditions the float approach has virtually disappeared when it comes to seeking large weights of bream. This is simply because the slow bait presentation so much desired by the species is virtually impossible with a float. The leger is by far the most successful method, used in conjunction with a quiver-tip bite indicator, the current invariably being too strong for a swing-tip to be of much use.

Another important difference in fishing the two types of water concerns the lie of the fish. Most moving-water venues are double-banked, a situation rarely encountered by the Fenland angler. Being natural watercourses, the faster flowing rivers tend to have their deeper parts in the middle, and this is where the fish seek sanctuary and where the angler must seek to catch them. This is opposed to the Fenland waters where the fish usually lie along the far bank where there is no more obvious loss of depth than elsewhere in the river.

For strong-moving waters, several strengths of quiver-tips will be needed, starting with something like ½₅in (40 thou) diameter and progressing upwards at approximately ¹⁄₁₀₀in (10 thou) stages. Ideally, these are set into a soft, through-action blank, making a rod of around 9ft with the solid glass quiver-tip accounting for some 18in of its length.

There are, of course, screw-in types available. But the match angler seriously attempting to catch fish on this type of water must furnish himself with several top joints as these are by far the most efficient.

For reel line, 2½lb is again recommended and hook lengths also follow a similar pattern to the Fenland choice in relationship to the baits being used. But a big diversion in approach comes in the field of groundbaiting. Whilst on the Fens, due to the stillness of the water, a light composition is required, on moving waters a heavy mix is necessary to get the bait down to the bottom without disintegrating. Remember, it has to be thrown distances of up to 30yd and then hit the water without breaking up.

Basically, the mix consists of a white bread, while very occasionally a little brown bread is added for extremely clear conditions. When mixed in the normal way, this will give all the weight needed to fulfil the requirements mentioned.

One big handicap with this type of bait consistency is the noise factor. And here it is up to the angler to look to the elements for a little help. On rougher, windy days, for instance, the noise of the groundbait hitting the water is largely eliminated by the choppy nature of the river, but on calm days the problem is not so easy to surmount. Here it is advisable to reduce the size of the balls of groundbait to the minimum practicable, and use twice as many. Very often there are motor boats and other craft on the river, and these can be turned to an angler's advantage as the unnatural disturbance caused by, say, a boat's propellers, can be useful as something of a decoy while the groundbait is thrown in. On hearing the approaching craft, the angler prepares one or two balls of groundbait so as to be in a position to deposit them amongst the turbulent waters immediately behind the passing boat.

Feeding is on a larger scale than for still water and probably about twice the amount is needed. An initial burst of some 2lb of groundbait, containing the usual additives of squatts and casters, is advised. Due to the current, a more regular feeding pattern is also demanded, something like a tennis-ball-size every ten minutes. The intervals can, of course, be varied to coincide with passing boats.

In moving water it is much more difficult to ascertain where groundbait is going to settle. Obviously, this won't be at the point of entry, and the answer to this really lies in experience. To give an example, on waters like the Severn, a rough guide we follow is, for every foot of depth the bait will travel a foot down the river. In other words, if the swim is 12ft deep, then the groundbait carpet will form some 4yd downstream from the point of entry.

A lead of $\frac{1}{2}-\frac{3}{4}$oz should be ideal in normal river conditions. If the current is extra strong due to rain then swan shots can be added to the length of line just above the bomb until a holding weight is achieved. The tail should be slightly shorter than that for the Fens, say about 4ft, with a shorter lead link, a maximum of 6in. The theory is, the faster the current, the shorter the link.

The cast is made to a point some three yards beyond the groundbait area, then the line is momentarily tightened to eliminate wind drift, and the lead allowed to sink quickly at its point of entry. The rod is then immersed as deep as possible in the river while a slow tightening action is performed, judging the movement of the lead so that it is positioned on the far side of the baited area. The rod is set at a 45 degree angle upstream with the tip some 2in above the surface. This should be adjusted in rough conditions, or on days of heavy boat traffic, as waves hitting the rod tip will make bite detection impossible.

On setting the rod, some two to three feet of slack line is let out in order to remove the extreme tension between the rod tip and the leger. This is aimed at obtaining more confident bites. The position should be held for two or three minutes, when movement of the bait is advisable. This involves picking up the rod and slowly dragging the terminal tackle for about 3ft along the riverbed. The rod is then placed back in the rest, remembering to take the tension out of the line, and the exercise is repeated three or four times in order to cover the area of groundbait.

Bites often materialize as the bait is settling after one of these adjustments. On indication of a bite, the angler is strongly advised to temper his action and introduce a positive but steady pull, rather than a quick jerk. On hooking a fish on these natural river courses, it is advisable to stand up so that full control can be exercised because the fish will be seeking every advantage it can gain from the root-strewn riverbed.

While in these respects there is a big difference between fishing still and moving waters for bream, in many other ways, such as the use of seasonal baits, the tactics are the same. Baits and hook selection relevant to this method are comparable to those for the Fens.

One other successful method of catching bream is by the use of the now popular swimfeeder. At a pinch, the same rod and indicator could also be used, but, to be honest, a slightly heavier design would be preferred.

Clive Smith with a nice bream

Because of the species' accepted interest in groundbait, an
open-ended feeder should be selected. One tip here is to keep
old feeders, those that become damaged, for instance, as the lead
strips are extremely useful when the current is pulling hard.
Simply clip on an extra length of lead strip. The feeder should
be connected to a short length of 3lb line with a No 12 swivel
tied some 3–4in from the feeder. The feeder is stopped by a
small shot, say a No 7, the required distance from the hook.

Although it means a bit of extra work, separate hook-lengths
should be tied at the required length of tail, as this will eliminate
slipping of the feeder if the shot is resting on the knot loop. A
3lb reel line is ideal with hooks tied to 1½lb in lengths of 18in,
24in with the occasional call for one of 36in.

Manual groundbaiting can also be carried out, even though
the feeder itself will be depositing amounts on the river bed. A
scaled-down version of the orthodox leger feed pattern can be
followed. The filling of the feeder is best done by putting the

84

thumb in the bottom end and packing sufficient groundbait to fill about a third of it. Neat squatts can then be added to fill another third of the volume, with a repeat of the groundbait at the top. Where casters are preferred these can be mixed equally in the groundbait, and the feeder can be filled in one go.

The position of the rod depends largely on the strength of the current. In very slow or still water, an orthodox position can be assumed, but the stronger the current the more vertical the position, lessening the resistance.

10 Chub

There are few similarities between the bream and the chub, though they are alike in one respect—they live and move in large shoals. And whilst this does not tend to provide an even match course, it does lead to spectacular match weights.

Methods and tactics for catching chub bear little comparison to those for bream. It is generally assumed that the chub is a shy fish. But this so-called shyness probably stems from the type of water it inhabits, often no more than 2ft deep, which makes any bankside movement clearly visible to the fish. Yet when conditions are ideal and a capable angler is 'sitting on' a shoal of chub, their confidence can be gained by careful feeding. After a time, in fact, they will become almost suicidal and this, in turn, leads to the big match scores. It must be stressed, however, that the fish can still easily be scared off and a reasonable amount of bankside discipline should be exercised if a fast catch rate is to be maintained.

Although chub are found living alongside bream in some of our slower-moving waters, they are much better known for favouring the more turbulent sections of our rivers. They also differ from bream in that they are at their best in clear conditions, whereas bream show their better form in slightly coloured water.

The chub is never happier than when intercepting a falling bait. This is the way it feeds naturally, as it must have done for thousands of years, long before anglers were heaping maggots and casters at it. It is the natural instinct of a chub to look upwards at overhanging branches of trees and anticipate a quota of feed from these sources. To simulate this feeding pattern, there is only one method—the slow-falling properties of an ideally suited float. And, over the past few years, the design which has established itself in this capacity is undoubtedly the waggler. Due to its light shotting pattern (see Fig 12) this float gives perfect bait presentation and, equally important, a silent, splash-free strike.

It is a common fault among anglers that, when using a waggler, because of an over-cautious approach, a model is chosen which is too light for the job. This leads to over-exertion of the cast with a resultant lack of consistency in direction and more interference in the area where fish are being caught. It is far better to choose a float slightly heavier than required to reach the desired spot, and over-cast, then draw back into the zone, thus eliminating any impact noise. This retrieving action has the added advantage of perfecting the tackle layout so that any drop bites can be seen as each shot registers its presence on the float. The shotting pattern for wagglers has been fully described in the chapter on floats and, as regards reel line, $2\frac{1}{2}$lb strength is ideal for almost every chub venue, with the possible exception of those waters where fish grow to extreme proportions.

The hook length depends greatly on the size of fish being caught, but in the majority of cases, with specimens up to the $1\frac{1}{2}$lb mark, a 1lb hook length can be vitally important, whilst for venues where the chub run just over the 2lb class, $1\frac{1}{2}$lb strength should be selected.

A diversion from this pattern is made when very fast water is being fished. It is common sense to suggest that a fish of around $1\frac{3}{4}$lb would exert twice the strain on the hook length in fast-flowing water than at a slow-moving venue. This also applies with hooks. It is generally accepted that the fine-wire variety is confined to slower rivers, whilst for faster flows the forged pattern is recommended.

In ideal conditions, when chub are intercepting a falling bait, the angler is obliged to feed little and often—a twenty-second cycle is recommended if manual feeding is possible, or if a catapult is employed it would have to be with each swim down. The important factor here is when to introduce the feed so that it will not destroy the all-important rhythm vital to the successful matchman.

There is a formula which can be followed loosely, but modified to suit varying conditions. For instance, in warm, early-season conditions, when chub are most active and taking the bait anywhere between the surface and the riverbed, the feed is best introduced at the end of a swim down. The strike is made at the bottom of the swim, a couple of turns made on the reel to eliminate any possible encroachment upon the downstream competitor, and the rod quickly set in the rest in a pre-determined position. The required amount of feed is then fired to the desired area, and the float cast among it. It is realized that this does entail a certain amount of time wastage, but the reader can be assured that it is by far the most efficient approach. When fish are taking just under the surface, a lot of false striking and snatching can result from them taking the bait immediately it enters the water, at a time when the angler is introducing his feed. This can lead only to extreme frustration.

Turning to colder conditions, this is when the chub feed much closer to the bottom and, although taking the bait on the drop, the action will be restricted to the last couple of feet or so. This allows the angler to utilize the time taken by the settling of the tackle to introduce the feed.

The amount of feed depends largely on the degree of response being gained from the fish. If it is a large shoal, and several fish are feeding, then twenty or thirty casters at a time is about right. On hard winter days, six or eight are often sufficient.

The ideal method of feeding is by hand, though in some conditions the only practical way is with the use of a catapult. We tend to feed three or four times every swim down, but use only the same amount of feed. This creates a natural situation of the feed falling through the water continuously, rather than the setting up of a regimented pattern. The big advantage with hand feeding is that it allows the angler two bites at the cherry—in the hot area of his swim he can place feed around his float at least twice, depending on the speed of the flow. With a catapult the angler is restricted to an entry of feed at the uppermost point of his swim. This obviously has the disadvantage of lessening the chance of a bite on the drop as the float moves out of this area. The chub shows a marked interest, too, in hempseed, and its introduction into the swim at the start of a match is recommended as it serves to hold the fish in the area. The amount to be used can be judged only from experience and by the degree of success it gains at a particular venue. On some waters it is more successful than others. A little hempseed can also be introduced in conjunction with the casters. A handful mixed into the pouch should be sufficient.

Another good tip for early- to middle-season chub fishing is the introduction of a few floaters into the feed. It does seem that when chub become preoccupied with surface feeding they lose their sense of caution to some degree. There is no valid reason for this, it is just a simple fact of fishing for chub.

When using the waggler the strike is important and this is where many anglers fall down. It is an extremely direct method of fishing and the bait can often be taken in a somewhat fearsome manner. Add to this the fact that the fish is going in the opposite direction, and the result of a sharp strike can only be a parting of company with the fish. All that is needed is a steady pull which leaves the angler time for adjustments at the point of contact. This float is ideally used when seeking chub on rivers up to 30yd wide with an unpopulated far bank offering a fair amount of cover. It can also be used with success in extremely windy conditions, especially when the blow is downstream.

On wider chub rivers, such as the Severn or Trent, where the far bank ceases to be a proposition, near-bank cover is all that is left to the angler. This is where a stick float becomes the obvious choice. It is ideally suited to presenting a close-in bait, lightly shotted so as to be attractive to a prowling chub. It offers the ultimate in bait presentation, and is most sensitive. Because of its slender design it is also, as far as double rubber floats go, quite silent.

It is obvious that fishing at this range will enable feeding by hand, and the same pattern can be followed as that described for the waggler. Although at times, especially on a river slightly above normal flow, the retarding of the bait gives best results, in normal conditions a free-running stick float is the downfall of many a chub.

The shotting capacity of the float is important and experience is needed to select the correct model without difficulty. A float which is too heavy will not present the bait in the free style which the chub likes. On the other hand, if it is too light in design it can become impossible to control and produce drag which immediately arouses suspicion among the chub.

It can be seen, therefore, that the right float is a prime objective of the match angler when fishing this type of swim. The routine we usually follow is to select a float which we believe will fit the bill, but use it merely experimentally at the start and waste no time at all in changing it to one more suitable, if it is necessary. It is so easy, and, in fact, is the case among a lot of anglers, to keep with a float chosen at the outset with apparent blind ignorance of the more suitable models in the float box. Remember, there are no extra prizes for the angler who chooses the right float first, only for those who catch the most fish!

The ideal line for a stick float is $1\frac{1}{2}$lb and a 1lb hook length is about right. Very often these will suit all requirements. In the type of water where the stick float is most suited, water of a more placid nature, chub of very large proportions are rarely encountered and, of course, the fish does not have the advantage of any strength of current.

The reader may have noticed that, when landing a fish which has been hooked at a distance while waggler fishing, it has usually been fairly co-operative when confronted with the landing net. When fishing closer in with a stick float, the chub will be very much more lively and in a far better state to seek bankside obstacles. Careful playing of the fish is most definitely needed, with the rod held in a high position. This tends to keep the fish looking upwards and not in the best position to see snags on the riverbed.

The big brother of the stick float, or to put it another way, the model chosen to fish at a similar distance but in faster waters, is the balsa variety. It is more buoyant and able to carry bulk shotting styles. The same feeding pattern can be applied as with the stick float, and a free run down the swim in good river conditions can produce deadly results. Because of the faster current, the reel line should be increased to $2\frac{1}{2}$lb, used with a $1\frac{1}{2}$lb BS hook length. The forged hook is recommended in this type of water.

With all three of these float-fishing styles, the hookbait would invariably be casters or maggots with the exception, perhaps, in the autumn when seed baits are at their most effective. This would not mean any great change in the selection of a float, or in shotting patterns. The stick float is ideal for seed baits, the major difference lying in the choice of hooks. This is especially the case where tares are being used as bait. Here, a much larger size hook is needed than may at first seem necessary. In fact, we recommend a size 14, fine-wire design, sometimes even a 12. This is because tares, even when thoroughly prepared by cooking, are probably the firmest bait in use. And for this reason a small-gape hook could be inadequate through being so sufficiently shielded as to prevent proper penetration.

Fig 19 The tare

The tare is a peculiar bait all round. The method of fixing it to the hook would appear to give little likelihood of catching fish (see Fig 19) but the reason for this type of presentation is to give maximum assistance in hooking the fish. If any other bait was fixed to the hook in this manner, the reader can be assured that the results would be very poor. But the fact is that normally hesitant and suspicious fish such as the chub, become suicidal when associated with the tare and determined to bite, irrespective of a bare hook!

Turning to hempseed, here a more obvious approach is made where hook sizes are concerned. An 18 is ideal in all but the most prolific sessions when a 16 could be substituted. Here again, a fine-wire design is recommended.

There are occasions, though they may be few, when wheat

is a killing bait for chub. Faster waters seem to suit this style best. Wheat is something of a poor relation in terms of results, though it can be a good bait in areas where wheat fields lie adjacent to the water.

If any bait has the right to claim distinction when it comes to catching big weights of chub or, for that matter, the largest stamp of fish, then the accolade must go to the humble bread. Although in recent years this bait has lost some of its popularity in match fishing, due to its properties of limited fish selection, it still remains a very efficient bait indeed. The problem is, of course, that by using bread an angler is ruling out catching those species which do not take this bait. But, when he is confident that there is a big shoal of chub in the swim, especially in streamy waters such as the Wye or Severn, then he just can't go wrong with bread on the hook.

A recommended approach in these wilder waters is to start the match using maggots until the resident species show themselves. If they turn out to be chub, especially the more substantial samples, those in the 2lb class, which seem to associate themselves with bread, then a change to this bait can be made.

Because bread is probably the most buoyant of all baits, a very unusual shotting pattern is needed, with the shot positioned close to the hook (see Fig 24 page 111). This also entails a large amount of shot; it can be as much as 7 or 8 swans, depending on the force of flow and distance to be cast. Because of the nature of the fish being caught, a substantial hook is also required, a size 8 to start and possibly larger later in the match. The line should be reasonably heavy, 3lb is the average choice, but in a more snaggy swim this could be increased to $4\frac{1}{2}$lb, especially when catching good-sized fish.

Bread fishing does call for a certain amount of groundbaiting. An all-white mix is ideal, laced with 2–3 pints of casters and a sprinkling of soaked bread.

Wasp grub fishing has many similarities to bread fishing, especially in terms of line selection, float sizes, and groundbait. The shotting pattern does vary slightly, but not the overall capacity (see Fig 20). Perhaps the biggest hurdle which the potential wasp grub angler has to clear is in casting his hookbait the required distance without it parting company from the hook.

Fig 20 Wasp grub set up

The secret here is to use an underarm, swinging cast, starting from a still, backward position. A slow but smooth build-up in speed is vital, reaching its peak at the full extension. This eliminates any jerky movements which are the sole cause of the grubs coming off the hook.

The number of wasp grubs used on the hook is of little importance, as a chub will accept any number. The only advantage of putting several on the hook is that it allows for the odd one to drop off en route to the swim. Wasp grubs are best hooked through the head, this being the slightly tougher end.

A vital factor in both wasp grub and bread fishing is the correct selection of the best line down the river to fish. Bearing in mind the shy nature of the chub, a point between mid-river and the far bank should be selected, and, in most cases, a careful study of the water will determine exactly where to choose.

Another method to which the chub is vulnerable is the swimfeeder style and this is dealt with in the section on swimfeeder fishing.

11 Roach

In terms of match fishing, the roach is the king among the species. There are few anglers, if any, who do not consider that to catch a bag of these wonderful fish is the highlight of the season. They would certainly top the poll if a census was taken.

Before the days of UDN (Ulcerative Dermal Necrosis), and, happily, again now, the roach was by far the most widespread of our fish, residing with every other known species. It can be found in abundance in the best bream waters of this country, and also in large quantities in the chub and barbel areas.

If a month was selected with which roach are mainly associated, it would be around the end of October. This is when the first frosts of winter seem to sharpen and condition them into a responsive mood. When conditions are right this is the time of year when sport can be guaranteed, making the roach the most predictable of all the species. Of the vast and varied types of water in which the roach is found, let us start with what is probably our first love, the medium-flowing rivers such as the Severn and Trent. It was on these types of water that the stick float was first formulated. And this has now become the accepted tool for the orthodox and successful approach to autumn roach fishing.

On moving water the roach can be found close in. The ideal position is a couple of feet on the moving side of the blend line (see Fig 21) and the angler should think of this position as the conveyor belt to the fish.

The roach is not one of the more robust types of fish and will always seek the somewhat quieter water having sufficient movement to provide a continual supply of passing feed. This is mainly applicable in the autumn and winter. In the summer months

94

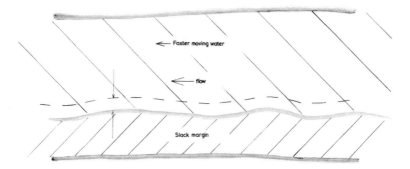

Fig 21 River showing slack margin 4–6ft wide and faster moving water. Fish on dotted line *2ft past* blend line

the roach, like many other species, can be found towards the centre of the river.

Similar to chub fishing, selection of the right stick float is of the utmost importance. It is so essential, in fact, that time should be allowed at the start of a match to ensure that the correct model is chosen.

The ideal line strength is 1½lb, and a 1lb hook length is invariably the best choice. By far the most popular bait for roach is the caster, and for this a fine-wire design hook, size 18 or 16, is recommended. There is a big tendency among anglers to regard this bait merely as a caster without any regard to the vast range of colours it passes through during the chrysalis stage. This is important, because the roach shows a marked preference for the dark-red coloured bait, the one in its later stages of production. There are probably two quite good reasons for this : in this late stage the caster is very crisp and can be easily crushed by a fish, and it has also developed air pockets, due to the formation of the fly inside it. This adds to the attractiveness of its presentation down the swim, as it lifts off the riverbed.

The roach is by far the most selective of our fishes, especially when developed to the 8–10oz mark. This means that a perfect hook caster is essential and is one reason why the fine-wire design is necessary. We go a step further by taking advantage of the barbless model. This allows the caster to be impaled without any barb passing through, thus obviating the large displace-

Ken Giles in action netting a fish

ment and resulting white blob, caused by interior leakage.

The roach demands the ultimate in bait presentation. In medium-flowing water a retarded bait is a must, and this is achieved by fishing over depth, sometimes as much as two or three feet, when a very slow or almost still bait is necessary. This is usually on hard frosty days, often in bad visibility. It is sometimes very hard to achieve this presentation, especially in snaggy swims, and one way to overcome this is by placing a number of micro-dust shots along the last three feet of line immediately above the hook. When the angler becomes familiar with the bed of the river, a little pressure on the float will easily lift the tackle over obstacles.

Hempseed has long been associated with roach, but in past years it has been better known as a hookbait. More recently it has taken on a role as an attractor bait, introduced to the swim in the initial stages of a match. If the angler is confident he is sitting on a good head of roach, then as much as 4 or 5 pints can be used. But where it is not known that roach are in the swim, then it is best to start with a smaller amount, and to feed at intervals, adjusting the quantities to the number of fish being caught. This bait, used as a ground feed, is unique in its method of introduction. All other attractor baits, such as maggots, casters or groundbait, are used on the little and often principle. But this new avenue with hempseed was opened up to us on the Continent. Some baits serve to be most attractive to fish as they fall through the water, even if it is intended to take them on the bottom. But hempseed gains little interest on its way down through the water; it is by far at its most effective when lying on the riverbed.

Before initially introducing hempseed into a swim, two or three trial runs down are recommended, to avoid throwing the feed on top of a bad snag. The feeding pattern for autumn roach is then about six to ten casters at very regular intervals, as many as five throws in a single swim down, which can sometimes be every ten seconds. A liberal sprinkling of hempseed is introduced to the caster bag, about 20 per cent of the total content.

This feeding pattern cannot be over emphasised. We fully accept the view that the same quota of casters could be introduced into the swim all at once. But this creates a very regimented pattern of feeding with enough evidence to suggest an angler's presence to the fish. By introducing six to ten casters, something of a single file situation is created and this is far more tempting to roach than a mass introduction of bait.

This theory has been proved several times by successes at the popular Stourport waters of the Severn where the roach are among the most cautious and suspicious, being mainly in that 10oz to 1lb stage. All too frequently their interest in the bait takes more than a little motivating.

We have enjoyed catches at this venue approaching 40lb of roach but it was on one occasion, in unfavourable river conditions, that Clive Smith found it necessary to scale down even this meagre feeding pattern still further, to minute proportions. He was at times introducing only a single caster at a time in an attempt to maintain the interest of the reluctantly feeding roach. But it paid off, and he went on to win the match easily with a weight of fourteen pounds, more than double the catch of the runner-up.

As the match progresses and the angler takes the odd fish, a picture will form as to where they are lying in the swim. This will depend upon where the bait is situated on the riverbed. These areas are usually dictated by the deviations of the river bottom. Often a slab of rock, or other silted-up obstacles, creates, with the help of the current, hollows which form ideal receptacles for the feed to become lodged as the current is diverted above them. The fish then move in for the accumulating bait. From this the angler can learn the area which should be concentrated upon. It is far better to cast a yard upstream, and pull out a yard downstream, of this area, than travel down the full length of one swim.

The methods described are for use in the more productive time of year for roach in reasonably favourable conditions. We then have the extremes, the warmer months of summer, not a good time for roach, and the very cold days of winter. During the summer the fish tend to move towards the middle, seeking the assistance of the current to present them with feed.

We hold the view that the roach gains the bulk of its feed at this time of year by sifting through the soft silt on the riverbed and removing particles of weed and tiny forms of life common to the season. This is evidenced by the black inky-like liquid found to be discharging from the vent when a roach is caught.

At this time of year it is likely that the angler has not set his sights specifically on roach, and considers them more of a make-weight species, probably in a match bag containing four or five different varieties. In varying rivers this can adjust itself. For instance, the Trent and Nene, and similar waters, can still produce a high percentage of roach during this period, though it generally follows in these cases that the rivers in question do have a rather low number of occupying species.

Because, very often, the fish are smaller at this time of year, a much finer approach is needed, and a pinkie or small feed maggot can be a killing bait. Cloudbait often works extremely well, while a size 20 hook to 1lb or even 12oz length can account for winning weights at a time when, invariably, scores of 3, 4 and 5lb are considered to be good.

Seeking out the current can often entail casts of up to 30yd and for this, of course, the waggler is the ideal float. Because of the sluggish nature of the rivers in summer a very fine insert

98

should be used in the float, and the one chosen should be capable of reaching the required distance easily, with the entry point about 2–3yd past the area being fished. This lessens disturbance and noise on still summer days.

If cloudbait is used, then it should be as light as possible, and if pinkies or squatts are added they should be mixed with each ball of groundbait, as required. Unless it is absolutely necessary to sink the line, it can be left on the surface, as with a 'top and bottom' float.

In winter, the roach, in common with other species, becomes quite immobile and requires a still bait, again presented along the blend line in moving water. A 2 swan link on a 4in length of line with a 4ft tail is ideal, used in conjunction with $2\frac{1}{2}$lb reel line and 1lb hook length.

The feed pattern is similar to that for stick float fishing, but vastly scaled down. The intake of food by the fish in these conditions will be very small and there is no point in putting in pint after pint of bait and so increasing the odds against a catch to an impossible degree. In still water the swing-tip is by far the best method, deeper water being the priority. In most cases, particularly on lakes, this will be at a distance.

Similar line proportions to those for moving water can be used, though the lead must be heavier, up to $\frac{3}{4}$oz. Feed must be kept to a minimum but has to be introduced in groundbait and this is best done with a catapult, thus achieving greater distance with very small pieces. Ideally, a piece of groundbait the size of a walnut, and containing three or four casters or maggots, should be introduced every twenty minutes after an initial feed of three or four pieces at the start of a match. As with summer fishing, the hook size should be kept as small as possible, epsecially when using maggots. On most occasions a size 20 is just right.

We now turn to canals, of which there are few, if any, in the British Isles which do not hold roach. They account for nine out of every ten winning bags, and most canal matches, summer or winter, can be won with 3 or 4lb of roach.

There are three popular canal baits—casters, maggots, and bread punch. The latter can very often be used in conjunction with the other two and, in common with other cereal baits, it is an instant producer. Best fished about 6in off the bottom, it is a wonderful bait with which to start a match. If it is to succeed there should be signs of a roach within ten minutes of the start. A size 20 hook to 1lb or 12oz length with a bread punch of $\frac{1}{8}$in diameter is preferred, and a No 10 shot placed some 9–10in from the hook, is all that is needed in the average canal with a depth of 2–4ft.

This method does call for a little groundbait, preferably the fine variety, to which a few coarse crumbs can be added. It is difficult to say whether brown or white is best, so we normally use a little of each.

We tend to fish the bread between the nearside and middle of the canal and follow this up by fishing caster or maggot well across towards the far shelf. Unlike bread, the caster or maggot is fished well on the bottom, especially in autumn or winter. This offers a perfect presentation where there is no evidence of a vertical line immediately above the hook, with the added

Clive Smith playing a fish

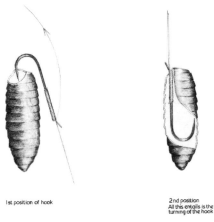

Fig 22 Hooking the caster

advantage that a foot or so of line on the bed of the canal helps to eliminate any drag which may be on the water.

If fishing caster, it is best to conceal the hook fully (see Fig 22), and, on most venues, a loose feed pattern is best carried out. The quantity of feed needed for a four-hour canal match would rarely reach a third of a pint.

Fishing the far shelf for roach, especially the larger samples, calls for much patience, as there would undoubtedly be a substantial time lapse before getting bites. In some cases this style entails sinking the line from rod tip to float, and this is not easy on canals because of the desirability of keeping the bait as near to the far bank as possible.

As in river fishing, the angler must not be frightened to use sufficient weight to be in full control of his tackle. Liquid soap or even fullers' earth used on an old line will help to sink it, and a small catapult will often be needed for accurate feeding.

Unlike most other forms of fishing, the canals vary very little during the seasons and a similar approach can be made in summer to that in winter, when roach are the quarry.

There is a growing feeling that a short rod is preferable for canal fishing. This can be $10\frac{1}{2}$–11ft, the advantage being that it maintains the perspective of casting and placing tackle on the narrower water.

12 Dace

Whilst roach inhabit pretty well all types of waters in this country, the dace, similar to chub, shows a marked preference for a moving environment. And though it is among our smaller varieties of coarse fish, it moves in king-size shoals which are nothing short of astronomical.

Some idea of this can be gauged from rivers where 50 and 60lb of dace are recorded in contests. Assuming that they run four to the pound, one can get the picture of just how many fish there are in a particular stretch of water, bearing in mind that it is quite commonplace for several anglers in a row to have similar big catches.

In years gone by the dace had something of a reputation for being a summer fish, but it is now considered to be the most consistent feeder and makes up winning catches right through the season. Ideal conditions for dace, as with bream, are when there is a tinge of colour in the river, preferably running off after a rise, and about two or three inches above its normal flow.

It shows no real preference as regards its area of residence in the river and can be found in equal numbers anywhere from the near bank to midstream. But it is important in terms of the match fishing potential that it is caught at a suitable distance from the peg. Similar to roach, it demands a good bait presentation, but it can be likened more to the bleak in its speed of interception of the bait.

It therefore follows that the type of tackle needed when fishing for dace must be such that it will give instant bite detection. In terms of the float, this is admirably filled by the stick design, and, although there are times when the waggler is preferred, it is, in general terms, functionally too slow for the sharp-feeding

102

dace. A 1½lb reel line and 1lb hook length is the ideal combination, a fine-wire hook being far more preferable than the forged variety.

When used for dace fishing, the shotting arrangement of the stick float does differ from that employed for chub and roach. The dace demands that the bait is presented in a lifting fashion and, to achieve this, two or three micro-dust shots, placed at 12in intervals, are ideal. When coupled with a varying degree of resistance applied to the float, the result is a lift and fall of the hookbait as it progresses down the swim. And, in the type of water inhabited by dace, it gives a simulation of loose-fed maggots or casters being introduced.

It may sound contradictory, but when dace are in their most co-operative mood, in terms of feeding, this is when it is most difficult to build up a good score. This is because they are often in a roving mood and wander out of the swim. Not so in harder conditions when they tend to reside in a small area all day.

The pattern of feeding is very important and is a major contributing factor towards catching large quantities of dace. If too little feed is introduced into the swim, the dace follow the line of feed to the source, and, as this is also the point of entry for the tackle, they are eventually scared away. On the other hand, if too much feed is used, then the enthusiastic dace will follow the bait down the swim until every last morsel has been consumed. Very often, this takes the fish well past the next angler downstream. And if his method of feeding is more efficient, then there will be little chance of getting the fish back to the upstream swim.

Correct judgement of quantity is therefore vitally important when dace fishing. It must be adequate enough for the dace not to have to move too near the entry point, and at the same time it must be consumed well within the length of the swim. A dependent factor is, of course, the number of fish being caught, but, by and large, the position in the swim where the dace are being caught is usually a good guide to how the feeding pattern is working out. If it is at the upper limit of the swim, then a larger amount of feed is needed, but if it is well down the run, then the quantity should be reduced.

The pattern of feeding applies largely to days when groundbait is not considered necessary—when the river is clear, or in very cold conditions when groundbait seems to have least effect. In coloured water, especially during summer or on mild autumn or winter days, groundbait plays a big part in catching dace. This is probably because it gives the visual attraction which is required.

The right type of groundbait is important. It must be finely sieved and of a cloudy nature. A mix of brown and white is ideal, in proportion of about two to one in favour of brown. A piece the size of a 50p coin should be introduced to the swim with each cast and, if maggots are being used on the hook, these should be added as necessary. Casters, of course, can be mixed on preparation of each measure of groundbait.

A 12ft rod is ideal for dace fishing and, essentially, a fine tip must be incorporated in its make-up. Too stiff a tip results in too many fish being lost off the hook. The dace shows a characteristic turn when hooked, perhaps better described as a propelling action when it seems to set itself in the shape of a banana and revolves at the end of the line. At this stage it is wrong to retrieve the fish rapidly. It will soon straighten itself out, and the retrieve can then be accelerated.

If a big weight is to be obtained, then disturbance caused by use of the landing net should be removed. Dace can quite easily be lifted from the water without a net, and it is well worth practising this, as anything short of a fluent action will result in the fish flapping about a short distance from the catching area.

The dace is instinctively a surface feeder and, during the three months enforced lay-off from fishing, because of the close season, it returns to its natural feeding method. This is why, during the first few weeks of a new season, good weights can be compiled by catching them on or near the surface. But this is also when they are at their sharpest and most difficult to catch. Bite indication by means of the float is quite useless, and the method most likely to succeed is that whereby a close watch is kept on the line between the float and hook. This short length of line should be greased at regular intervals to help visual bite recognition.

Incidentally, in this type of fishing, the term 'float' simply means a casting weight. Most efficient is a piece of hardwood unpainted to allow it to absorb water, giving additional weight to assist casting (see Fig 23).

Floating casters are an ideal feed, but, should the dace become suicidal, then a maggot can be used on the hook and two or three fish taken without need to change the bait. A roach pole is ideal if the fish are sufficiently close in to allow its use, and a donkey tip is much preferred to elastic as it eliminates the bouncing of the fish when it comes to land.

If the dace are at too great a distance out from the bank to allow for pole fishing, then there is no alternative but to use a rod and reel.

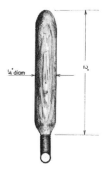

Fig 23 Surface float for dace

13 Barbel

None of the species so far dealt with has been strongly linked with any of our four seasons. The barbel is different. This whiskered variety shows a marked preference for summer and early autumn conditions when it comes to feeding, and in this it does bear some similarity to that prima donna of the non-match-fishing section of our sport, the tench. This is also most active during the warmer weather, though there is nothing to suggest that the environmental surroundings are responsible for this. The two species, in fact, reside in totally different types of water.

The barbel is also distinctive in being probably the least widespread of the sought-after match fish in this country. It is mainly associated with the Hampshire Avon, a river which, twenty years ago, housed the majority of our barbel population, and other waters such as the Thames, Yorkshire Swale, and more recently the Severn. The development of barbel in the Severn, where they were introduced from the Kennet in 1954, has been nothing short of amazing and there is no doubt that it is now the finest barbel river in the country.

In good conditions spiralling Severn match weights of around the 100lb mark can be expected in a five-hour match. In general, though, it is fairly safe to assume that a minimum of 50lb of barbel will be needed to win a fair-sized open on the Middle Severn. But it must be said that if the right angler draws one of four or five noted swims at the right time of year, in the right conditions, then there seems to be no limit to the potential weight which he could put together.

The class of fish which produce the regular winning catches are undoubtedly those in the 2–3lb range. These tend to make up the biggest shoals and they remain resident in a swim for long periods. The larger fish, and these can run into double figures, tend to shoal in much smaller quantities.

It can safely be assumed that the 2–3lb barbel make up the bulk of the parent stock, and it is around August or September before they reach prime condition after spawning. This coincides with the period of the heavyweight catches which are so common in barbel matches. This theory is party borne out by the fact that, early in the season, the stamp of fish which predominate among the catches are in the 1lb range, and not old enough to spawn. These early-season fish show a preference for a float-presented bait and feed similar to chub of the same size. They will intercept a bait on the drop in a manner completely divorced from their reputed characteristics as bottom feeders. Evidence of this can be gained by watching a shallow swim known to be inhabited by barbel, where small fish will be seen topping frequently all through the day.

Because of the shallow water preferred by barbel, there is little doubt that the best float to use is the waggler. It offers everything that is required in catching these fish. Some of the swims can be as little as a foot deep, presenting an impossible task for a top and bottom attached float, for three main reasons. Firstly, it is well nigh impossible to cast a tackle rig, set for so shallow a depth, the required distance without incurring tangles. Secondly, the force needed to set a hook in a tough-mouthed barbel can only result in top and bottom attached tackle leaving the water on the strike and finishing yards upstream. And thirdly, the noise factor, when fishing in only a foot of water, when the intercepting fish is close to the float can be disastrous when using a double rubber float. To all these problems, the waggler is the complete answer.

Line selection is different when fishing for barbel. The angler considers himself first, and the fish comes second! The reason for this is, simply, that the barbel is one of the boldest feeders and shows not the slightest alarm at a reasonably stout line. The assessing factor must be the degree of control capable of being exercised on the line by the angler. For instance, it would be all right fishing with a 5lb BS line, close in, but extremely hard to work this tackle at a distance of, say, 30yd in a downstream wind! The ideal strength is 3lb BS which is invariably heavy enough to handle most fish and at the same time fine enough to retain all the attributes expected of the tackle when downstream winds can be a major factor.

A size 14 forged hook carrying two or three casters or maggots is ideal, and, in shallower swims, a No 8 shot placed 8–10in from the hook and set 1–2ft over depth, depending on weed, is all that is needed. The weight of a size 14 hook provides just that little extra help in placing the tackle on the riverbed. In deeper swims, up to 5–6ft, a No 6 shot halfway between the No 8 and the float, would be ideal. This method is generally used in conjunction with loose feeding as the barbel seems to show little interest in groundbait, looking only for the more wholesome offerings.

A catapult is a must, and it is essential to work up a steady feeding rhythm. Because of the speed of the current, permanent contact with the float must be maintained and this means that the feeding exercise has to be done at the end of the trot down. Once a swim is finished, it is best to reel back 3–4yd of line, drop the rod in a well positioned rest, then fire the required amount of feed to the point in the swim where it is needed. The rod can then be picked up, and the tackle retrieved. A check on the hookbait, replace if required, and the tackle can then be cast smartly back to the fishing position.

In this type of fast water, so long as the line is upstream, there is little need to exercise restraint and the tackle can be allowed to run freely through the swim. If the float disappears, a fast pull should be given. If the cause of the strike was not a fish, then it is possible that the float will not have moved too far off its course, making it unnecessary to retrieve the tackle fully. In this case the line can simply be released and allowed to trot down the rest of the swim—always with an eye kept open for the next disappearance of the float. Finally, when selecting the shot capacity of a 'waggler', the angler should always lean towards the heavy side. Not only will this assist with casting, it will give the tackle a form of independence in this more turbulent water.

Though this is the most popular type of barbel water, there are much deeper swims and these often contain the larger fish. These bigger samples, in fact, seem to prefer the margins of the rivers, making the choice of float a top and bottom design.

Dependent on the strength of flow, this can be either a stick or a balsa variety and, as with the waggler, a 3lb line is recommended, with a size 14 hook.

Barbel have an amazing capacity for bait, and this necessitates an angler carrying as much as a gallon on some occasions in order to satisfy the demand. This can comprise casters, or maggots, or some of each, and there is no hard and fast rule concerning proportions. As a very rough guide, the caster is usually the best bait to use in conjunction with a float, and the maggot with a swimfeeder, a method which will be dealt with later in terms of fishing for barbel. A supply of hempseed is also recommended as barbel do show a definite liking for this bait and it serves as an ideal attractor on the bed of the river. Some 3–4 pints is quite an adequate supply for a match.

Another popular bait for barbel is luncheon meat, used either straight from the tin, or in paste form. Paste is perhaps to be preferred as the tinned meat can vary a lot, depending on temperature. On very hot days, in fact, it can become almost

Ken Giles after one of his many victories, with the Avon Rose Bowl

unusable because of its soft nature, while in late autumn and winter it hardens to such an extent that it protects the taking fish from the hook! To make a good paste, the meat should be removed from the tin and pulped by hand, adding a little flour. To obtain the required consistency, the mix should be tested by taking a hook, say size 8 or 10, and placing on it the required amount of meat and spinning it round by hand. If the mixture is not sufficiently stiff, then the hook and paste will part company, and more flour is required. The mixing is best done at home, before a match, and the bait is suitable for either float or leger fishing.

When float fishing with luncheon meat for barbel, the float needed is a balsa design and the method is similar to bread fishing for chub with the bulk of the shot placed some 12–18in from the hook. The float capacity is determined by the casting distance, but it is unwise to use a float capable of carrying anything less than 2 swans. A 3lb line is ideal and a No 8 or 10 forged hook is recommended. A shotting pattern to follow is given in Fig 24.

A complementary feed to luncheon meat is casters, used in the same proportions as though they are being used on the hook.

Of all the heavyweight catches made in match fishing, the swimfeeder can rightly stake a claim to being responsible for the vast majority. This is not to say that it is the most enjoyable type of fishing, but, when sitting on a big shoal, it is often the most direct and efficient method.

A stout rod is essential for this type of fishing, and this has been described in a previous chapter. The best reel to use is an open-face design, preferably one of the ball-bearing models, and it should be filled with 8lb monofilament line.

Anglers often get confused when told that we use lines of this BS and are wrong in thinking that the reasoning behind it is to catch fish of a similar weight. The explanation is, simply, that it has to be strong enough to work with a feeder loaded with enough lead to anchor it in the middle of the river in fast water, and, loaded with maggots, weighing anything up to 4oz. It has to be cast the required distance and, when the fish takes the bait, the feeder has to be instantly bypassed in order to make contact with the barbel. A lesser BS line would show a large

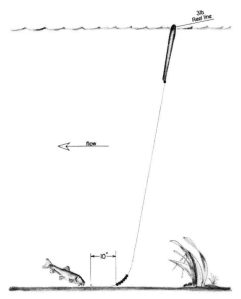

Fig 24 Bread set up

degree of elasticity, making it much more difficult to get results.

Because of the cross-sectional area of the line, as much of it as possible should be out of the water. The rod is best pointed upwards at an angle of about 45° (see Fig 25). The feeder itself should be of a large cylindrical design with a link swivel fitted directly to it, or, as the authors prefer, tied in direct to the reel line (see Fig 26 A, B, C). The bite indication does not suffer in any way and it eliminates the annoying habit of the feeder sliding away down the line on the occasions when the rod tip is lower than the butt.

The actual hook length should be 1ft to 2ft, the shorter distance being brought into use on the more prolific days when the hook can be tied direct to the reel line. In these situations a 4lb hooklength is about right to start with, and from the results obtained the angler can decide whether a change, either up or down, is needed.

At the start of the season a large forged hook, a 12 or even a size 10, can be used with up to three maggots as the offering. But as the season progresses it will become necessary to drop

111

Fig 25 Position for feeder-fishing

down to a size 16, or even 18, as the fish become more hesitant in taking the feed.

These smaller size hooks should always be the strongest available, with a breaking strain never below $2\frac{1}{2}$lb. A single maggot or caster can be very effective on hard days.

A tip, when feeder fishing, is to start off with a model having the bottom row of holes enlarged to somewhere near twice their normal size. This helps in getting a good quota of feed in the swim in the initial stages of a match. Once the barbel are resident, then the tackle can be adjusted, if it is thought necessary.

Barbel bite indication is very positive and rod tip movement going up to the unimaginable proportion of 2ft can be experienced. As previously stated, in this situation a quiver-tip is more of a hindrance than a help.

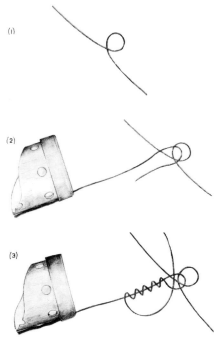

Fig 26a Swimfeeding. Method of feeder attachment. Make loop in line, pass feeder through, then twist line round itself 5–6 times. Pass through itself and pull tight

Normal leger fishing for barbel can be very deadly, especially in slightly coloured water, with either meat, maggots, or casters on the hook. Because of the nature of the water, a flat lead is preferred with meat fishing. A 10in link with a 20in hook length is ideal, and 3lb line in most cases. The best position for the rod is upright, held physically without the use of a rod rest.

The lead weight should be just heavy enough to hold the current so that an inquisitive fish moving the lead only slightly will, with the assistance of the current, trigger off a definite movement. This often results in 'flick-back' bites which, in this type of fishing, outnumber the pluck bites by four or five to one. The ideal legering rod is a stiffish action 9ft design, and a quiver-tip is advisable.

Legering with maggots and casters is a method used mainly

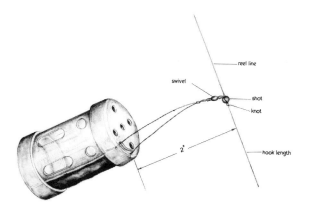

Fig 26b Tie knot in reel line, slide feeder and swivel above knot then place BB shot above knot. Tie loop for hook or hook direct. *Note* : If loop required make sure it falls below feeder to avoid tangle (see Fig 26a)

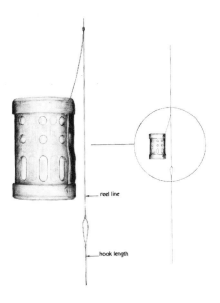

Fig 26c Feeder in position

towards the end of the barbel season when the fish are becoming lethargic and show less interest in the feed. A 3lb line is ideal, but a size 16 forged hook to 2.6lb bottom will probably make the difference between having no bites and inducing a fish to feed. The type of swim where this tackle is used is the deeper-flowing water where the feeding habit continues until about October and November, making barbel fishing still a practical proposition. In this type of swim the position of the rod can be more orthodox, 45 degrees upstream, and low on the water. And here again, a selection of quiver-tips is required.

14 Bleak

Among our smaller fish varieties with match-winning potential is the bleak, but this challenge is only applicable in certain areas, notably the southern half of the country and more especially the south east. The importance of bleak is not only as a possible winner, though. It has assumed a very vital role since the innovation of the points system in the National Championship and other similar team events. Very often even only one of these tiny silver fish can be worth its weight in gold in the poorer sections of a contest, sections which often determine the final outcome of a match.

Some years ago, when 10lb was an exceptional match weight, bleak played a big part in scores at this level. These small fish were possibly more widespread in those days. For instance, in our own local waters of the Lower Severn, once noted for its hoardes of bleak, there has been a considerable lessening in the numbers over the past few years. It is very true that, with the much larger present-day catches of other species, the true potential of bleak has possibly been ignored. When individual results have been sought the outcome has, therefore, been something of a mystery.

Basically, there are two ways of catching bleak. There is the situation where they are prolific in a water and a winning catch of, say, 10 or 12lb is on the cards, when the method would be by the greased line approach. Or there is the water to be fished where they are in much lesser quantities, in conditions often associated with the avoidance of the dreaded dry net, or perhaps the hard winter matches where 2lb might be a good weight. Here, a more orthodox form of fishing is pursued.

First, let us take the case where there are plenty of bleak and they are showing themselves on the surface, rising to the angler's feed. This is when they are easiest to catch, and they show little sign of recognizing danger. A contributing factor to this situation must be that their demand for feed has not been satisfied, forcing them to challenge each other for the bait.

The key to obtaining and maintaining this state of affairs is the actual feed which should be offered to the fish. It is of little use using bait of only one type, either maggots or casters. This would give a uniform rate of fall through the water, especially in the case of maggots, and would result in the hookbait being betrayed through falling at a faster rate, due to the weight of the hook. It is important, therefore, that the fall rate should be inconsistent, and the ideal feed to achieve this is a small supply of ordinary maggots, some old and some new, a few pinkies, and squatts when obtainable, together with some casters in varying stages of maturity. And with the latter it is important that the floater should not be neglected.

It does no harm to crush a few of the baits when feeding. Not only does a bait menu of this nature offer the perfect variation in drop rate, it provides the angler with an ideal supply of change baits.

It has not gone unnoticed that an opportunity sometimes arises where the bleak show an interest in floating casters, and a switch to these on the hook can bring a much larger sample of bleak. There is also the added advantage that a larger hook can be brought into use.

Talking in terms of a double-figure catch of bleak, a pint of feed, as described, is more than sufficient. When used in conjunction with a double pocketed apron in which hookbaits can be kept separately, the whole operation is made both speedier and more efficient.

The manner of introducing the feed is important. The correct approach is to introduce a pinch of feed every ten or fifteen seconds over an area of four or five yards, reducing it to two or three morsels, aimed at the hook, when the fish become more co-operative. This can almost guarantee a fish every put-in. During these prolific periods, larger fish can often be found by casting the tackle to the outer area of the shoal, and this is also the best way to prevent disturbance to the main body

117

of fish. It is, in fact, unwise to make two successive casts in the same place, hence the 5yd area.

On the more abundant days, a roach pole is an ideal tool for the job, used in conjunction with a soft top. This is much preferred to elastic, which introduces bounce into the operation and makes a clean catch difficult. A long, soft top, about 18in, tapering to something like ⅟₃₂in (30 thou) diameter at the tip is ideal. The pole should be the take-apart design rather than the telescopic model, to ensure that the matchman can follow the shoal of fish as it moves towards mid-river, as inevitably happens.

Starting with a length of about 13ft, a joint of the pole can be removed when the fishing is really fast. A 1½lb line is recommended, with 1lb hook length and a barbless size 18 hook for the best general approach. In this type of fishing, the float is of little importance in terms of bite indication. It merely gives the necessary weight to place the tackle where desired. A recommended float is a piece of hardwood dowel about ³⁄₁₆in diameter and 1½in long, torpedo-shaped at one end, with an ordinary attachment ring at the other. It is left unpainted for the very good reason that it absorbs water and assumes a low profile in the water, thus making it more difficult for the wind to disturb it and so make the bait move unnaturally. It is worth noting that, when the float hits the water, the resultant splash often produces an instant bite as the bleak confuses the splash with one of its fellows.

A wide-top keep-net is absolutely necessary; 24in diameter is ideal. This should be placed in a table top position, offering the largest possible area to catch any dropped fish which, in this style of angling, can often be a deciding factor. Though in most other methods of match fishing we prefer a standing position, the governing factor when seeking bleak is the type of cover available, depth of water, and distance at which the fish are being caught.

We now turn to fishing for bleak in the less plentiful waters. In this situation there would not be any challenge by the fish for feed as they are very selective and demand the finest degree of bait presentation. In these conditions the most difficult task is to try and find the depth at which the bleak are resident in the water. For reasons best known to the fish, they prefer to be at one level and it very often happens that, after a fruitless hour or so, variation of the tackle can produce bites. When fish are contacted, whether by means of a bite or a chewed maggot, this depth should be maintained for a period of time during which the angler should confidently expect results.

These are the days when the fish wander over a large area. Even in flood conditions, when an extra 2ft of water is going down river, they find little difficulty in holding in midstream. Here, the limited approach offered by a pole would be quite useless for a considerable part of the match when the fish would simply be out of range. Ideally, the angler should set up a take-apart pole and a tip-action match rod. As in the previous method, $1\frac{1}{2}$lb reel or pole line is preferable, with 1lb hook length, and, because of the difficulty in tempting the fish, a size 20 barbless hook is preferred.

The major difference between the two styles is the float. Unlike the previous method, where it is merely an aid to casting, here it assumes its orthodox use. A small waggler type is ideal as this can often be thrown a fair distance when required, with no risk of tangles. It would be hard to achieve with a top and bottom design, bearing in mind the type of shotting needed to suit the style. After testing many types of float for this style of fishing, we have yet to find one to match the fine-tip porcupine carrying two to three BB shots. It shows great independence when negotiating fast-moving water where there are often varying currents.

When using a pole, a small top and bottom porcupine float with a flattened top carrying two No 8s and a No 10 spread at equal intervals, with the No 10 about 8in from the hook, should be adequate. With this sensitive type of float, an inserted ring at the top is preferred to the float rubber. This removes the possibility of the float sitting up in the water with the float cap supported by the surface.

When seeking odd fish in still waters, such as the Welland or Nene, say, during a national, a porcupine float, because of its weighty property, can be cast fair distances and still be in perspective. A No 10 shot placed 12–14in from the hook, with the remainder of the shots on either side of the float, is all that is required.

Because of the small numbers of interested fish, a minimal quantity of feed is required. There is no advantage to be gained from using a large variation of baits, in fact, a mixture of pinkies and larger maggots will suffice. These can be fed in two's and three's about every thirty seconds.

Clive Smith about to make a cast

15 Gudgeon

Although probably the most widespread of all our coarse fish species, in terms of its match fishing potential the gudgeon is limited to canals and the odd lowly populated, slow-moving river venues.

It has a mystifying peculiarity in being able to completely 'lose itself', for no apparent reason, from a particular venue. It is accepted that a lot of fish do this on a seasonal basis. For instance, roach are noted for showing up best in the autumn, bream early in the season. But gudgeon follow no true pattern. One year they can be in evidence at a venue during the winter, and the following season completely reverse the situation. A good example of this came in the Trent 'Nationals' of 1975 and 1976. The 1975 match was, to a large extent, decided by the vast gudgeon population in the river. But the following year the contest was notable for their absence, as, on a fast-rising river, anglers sought in vain to catch one or two of these points-gaining fish.

It is on the canals that the gudgeon really shows its potential; and nowhere more than in the Midlands. There are several venues in the area—Staffs–Worcester Canal, Oxford Canal, Grand Union or Shropshire Canal, to name a few—where on many occasions gudgeon have decided the complete prize list. With weights ranging up to 5lb, sport is brisk and always interesting. Successful fishing for gudgeon demands a lot of skill and perfect bait presentation. But, equally important, the gudgeon is a fish which gives sport, albeit in varying degrees, to the less accomplished angler, thus making it a type of fishing which is satisfying for everybody.

A factor in the larger exploitation of gudgeon has been the

increased popularity of the pole and the finely balanced tackles associated with it. These small fish are usually found at the foot of the bankside slope around the nearside bank, and are ideally suited to this type of tackle set-up.

A take-apart pole is best as its ability to be extended gives the advantage, firstly, of being able to follow the shoal of fish as it creeps farther out from the bank, and also, if an unexpectedly large fish is encountered, such as a perch or a tench, the extra length can be vitally important.

We always use a crook and elastic, rather than a donkey tip, as this is an insurance when hooking the larger fish. A 1½lb pole line is preferable, solely because it has the advantage of being able to adjust shots with reasonable confidence, with a hook length of ¾lb. A size 22 barbless fine-wire hook with a sharpened point is just about right for the job. In the case of bloodworm fishing, there is a special model of hook available, red in colour and made with an exaggerated shank. A little bit of extra attention paid to the hook is of benefit, not only for positive hooking of the fish, but also to facilitate the attaching of baits without bursting. This is especially applicable to bloodworms.

For shotting, a standard pattern is usually followed, ie, a No 12 about 4in from the hook with two to five No 8s—always accepting that most canals vary in depth from 2–5ft, ie, one No 8 per foot of depth—placed 12in from the hook. The depth at which the hook is set is dependent upon the bait being used. For bloodworms, for instance, it should be fractionally off the bed of the canal, and with maggots, ie, squatts and pinkies, it should lie 1–2in on the canal bed.

The bloodworm, used in conjunction with jokers, reigns supreme when it comes to catching gudgeon. Nowadays this bait can be purchased commercially, and the requirements for a match are a pint of neat jokers and sufficient bloodworms for the hook. The groundbait used in this type of fishing has been described in a previous chapter and its introduction into the swim is rather unusual, and worth mentioning.

This is a case where the groundbait is effective only on the canal bed, in complete contrast to other situations where it has a degree of attraction as it falls through the water. This means that the quicker the operation is carried out, the better, and the right procedure is to introduce the feed at the start of a match. It has been proved that this somewhat drastic measure does not put the fish off for very long and a brisk catch rate is often built up within ten minutes or so of the operation being carried out.

The quantity of groundbait put down depends largely on the fish population in the canal, and a good guide is to assess as accurately as possible what the winning weight will be, and allow one lot of groundbait, tennis-ball size, and laced with $\frac{1}{4}$ pint of jokers for each 1lb of that estimated weight. In other words, if the forecast is that 2lb will win the match, two balls of groundbait should be used, if it is 3lb, three balls, and so on. But in shallower depths of, say 2–3ft, it is recommended that smaller balls should be used, say, half the size, but double the quantity, to bring it up to the same amount.

After the initial introduction of groundbait into the swim, further small balls of groundbait, about the size of a 10p piece should be used for 'topping up' when sport tends to slow down. But when fish are feeding strongly, groundbait should never be used.

The bloodworm is probably the hardest of all baits to fix to the hook, partly because of its jelly-like make-up and, of course, its smallness. This is where a sharpened hook pays dividends. The hands must be kept clean and, for this purpose, facilities should be kept readily available. The bloodworm is taken between the forefinger and thumb of one hand with the green head protruding. Taking the hook between the forefinger and thumb of the other hand, the two are then offered together in much the same way as striking a match, only more slowly.

Squatts and pinkies are normally used in conjunction with each other, the squatt being complementary to the pinkie. When the going is particularly hard, the squatt can also be an ideal change bait on the hook.

In this case the tackle set-up is identical to that for fishing bloodworms. The ideal float is a top and bottom attached balsa bristle, or a small porcupine. The porcupine is best flatted off at its thickest point, and a gold ring fixed about $\frac{1}{8}$in from the top (see Fig 27).

One difference comes in the introduction and composition of

123

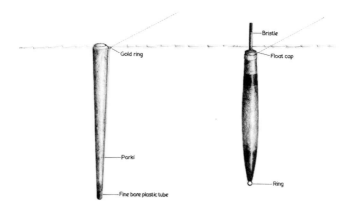

Fig 27 Pole Float

the groundbait. A cereal bait is used in this case, very fine brown bread, and it is introduced into the swim on a little and often principle. A portion the size of a 5p piece every minute or so, containing two or three squatts, would be ideal for the average venue. This can, of course, be adjusted when there is either an excessive amount of fish, or when the population is sparse. On average, a pound of dry feed is usually more than enough for a match, with a half pint of squatts and sufficient pinkies for the hook.

16 Swimfeeder fishing in Slower Waters

In the section on barbel fishing, the more robust approach of the swimfeeder was described. But, in all types of angling, variations have to be made to suit both conditions and the species being sought. And this is applicable to the swimfeeder.

A more delicate approach with a smaller type of feeder, used in conjunction with finer lines, is demanded in the slower-moving waters where fish have more time for inspection. This is more exaggerated in the winter months when match weights tumble to rock bottom and there is little opposition to the feeder, especially at venues holding odd chub and bream.

In contrast to the heavyweight rod, previously described for barbel fishing, a more orthodox leger rod, incorporating a quiver-tip, is required for the quieter waters. And if the angler is fortunate enough to have a wide range of tackle at his disposal, then a rod slightly stiffer than the conventional soft top design is preferred.

A 3lb reel line is definitely advised as the feeder still has to be moved before contact is made with the fish. And a $1\frac{1}{2}$lb hook length is most realistic, used with a forged hook, the size of which depends on the species most likely to be contacted.

The length of tail also depends on the species—bream demanding the longest, up to 3–4ft. For other types of fish, anything from 12–18in should suffice, the general rule being, the more eager the fish are to feed, the shorter the tail.

Selection of the right size of feeder is important and it is necessary to obtain a correct balance. The same thought should be given to this as to selection of a lead for leger fishing, to ensure that it is just sufficiently weighty to hold the bed of the river.

The feeder should be connected to a 3in link via a swivel. This is stopped the required distance from the hook by a small shot. In most commercial feeders the size of the hole is inclined to be rather small and it is best to open this up to about $\frac{3}{16}$in.

The rod position is dictated by the speed of the current. The slower the water, the lower the rod, arriving at the situation where, in still water, the normal orthodox leger position is adopted. This is because the cross-sectional force of the current on the line is non-existent, so there is no advantage in exposing the line to whatever wind pressure there might be.

The angler is advised to hold the rod, supporting it on a single rod rest position some 3ft from the tip. In this slower type of water, the tackle can be left in the water for a lengthy period of time, in winter as long as ten minutes, and on very still water this can be extended even farther. It may be necessary to assist the bait out of the feeder by giving short, jerky pulls on the line occasionally, especially when water temperature is low.

For bream fishing, the open-end type feeder is preferred, as it incorporates the use of groundbait, ideally suited in conjunction with squatts. When packing these it is best to have the groundbait completely neat, packing one end first, adding the squatts separately, then finishing off the job by packing the base end. For other species of fish, the block-end type is preferred, used with neat feed, either maggots, casters, or both.

The position of the feeder in the swim is important if clear bite indication is to be achieved. It is best situated slightly downstream of the angler at an angle of about 10 degrees. The tackle should be set, then a slight slackening-off operation performed to ensure that the tip is at its most sensitive.

The whole method is dependent upon a smooth rhythm being maintained and this will undoubtedly be centred around the feeder filling operation. An ample bait utensil is required. If adopting a standing position, a large apron pocket is ideal for the bait, but, if sitting, then a half biscuit-tin clipped to the front of the creel offers a good area.

Always bait the hook first, and follow this by filling the feeder. In this way it prevents maggots finding their way out of the feeder while the hook is being baited.

126

PART THREE
Match Fishing

17 Team Fishing

The last few years have seen the emergence of several top-class team events throughout the country and these have been of definite advantage to the match angler in considerably sharpening his competitive approach. Let us take a look at some of the benefits which accrue from this team fishing aspect.

First and foremost, team fishing creates a high degree of discipline, much greater than when the matchman is individually motivated. A common failing in an otherwise good angler fishing on an individual front is his lack of fight when drawing an average sort of peg. With the limited amount of knowledge he has been able to obtain, it is so easy for him to reason that the fish are just not there in the quantity required to gain a place in the prize list. Not so in team fishing, however, where the good squad man knows it is vital to pull his weight and see out the match to the bitter end, despite the nature of his peg. This invariably leads to 'no hope' pegs bringing some degree of success. To do a good job for one's team from this sort of swim brings terrific satisfaction. And the overriding bonus is that when drawing a similar type of peg in an individual contest, the experience gained from team fishing convinces the competitor that no peg is a completely hopeless case.

Another big advantage from team fishing is the swopping of information concerning methods and ideas. These would probably have been on the secret list if it was an individual match. But where other teams have to be beaten, then collective skills are necessary, and that old cliché, two heads are better than one, definitely applies. When as many as twelve heads are pooling their knowledge, it makes for an excellent basis on which to adopt a wide-ranging approach to a match.

It is far from easy to build a successful team. The majority of events call for teams of twelve anglers, and to mould together such a number of competent matchmen can take several years. Most of the major team matches are now decided on a points basis, and this makes a team as strong as its weakest link.

The type of angler to look for is the one with plenty of experience behind him, and, at the same time, still physically capable of doing the job in hand. He will be able to relate his knowledge to others, and, for this sort of communication to take place, it is important that regular meetings are held.

It is possible that these spokesmen will be few in the early stages, but confidence soon grows and eventually every member of the team will be contributing to the discussions. This will all help to bring about a friendly understanding among the members, which is so important. No angler should ever be frightened of putting forward a point, however small it may seem, for fear he may be ridiculed. Very often matchwinning plans are developed from these obscure reasonings—it is never the obvious that wins a match.

An angler's skills don't become apparent in one or two matches, and, when assessing potential team members, they should be observed over a period of time. Furthermore, top-class anglers will not join a team which has no track record, and a squad must be at least half-way to being successful before it can hope to attract the matchfishing cream.

In choosing a side, a team captain has to be something of a psychoanalyst. For instance, a controversial type can do much to unbalance a side. On the other hand, some anglers are very reserved and need encouragement to come forward with ideas. All this hinges on formulating a friendly atmosphere.

Satisfaction with a team should never be totally reached. A careful blend of youth and experience is the ideal, and the respect for the captain must be 100 per cent, as a squad policy is unquestionably the best method. With a surplus of up to three anglers over the required number, it does entail the unenviable task of deciding on the final twelve for the team. This is where respect for the captain's judgment becomes obvious. His decision must be final if the team is to go forward purposefully.

It is important that financial commitments should be shared

and consideration given to the differing circumstances of the team members. A man should not be embarrassed by his financial position to the extent that he is reluctant to come forward and contribute his efforts.

Let us take a major contest, such as a National Championship, and go through the build-up to such an event. It is advisable that the selection of the squad should be made as soon as possible after the previous year's event. This gives the advantage that corresponding river and weather conditions will be prevailing at the time of selection, and an early indication of what can be expected in twelve months' time can be gained by a study of Press reports of events at the big match venue.

During the next four or five months, an understanding should be developed among the squad members with a very general approach to the big event. Those with first-hand knowledge of the venue (we have to bear in mind that the match water might be 200 miles away) will be those to put forward most of the information, and this will create a picture in the minds of those members with little experience of the water.

Although, obviously, no policies can be formulated at this early stage, a general acclimatization is well worth having. Similar local pieces of water can be looked at, and types of floats and other tackle tried out. At this time, too, other events organized shortly prior to the big match should be sought, and tickets obtained, together with any information relative to possible practice on the water. It very often happens that if these moves are left too late, all tickets are sold, and the chance of a work-out at the venue is lost.

It is not essential to visit the particular venue too soon before the match as, of course, conditions corresponding to those likely to apply on contest day will not be forthcoming. This practice and the formulation of the final plan must be condensed into a three-week period immediately prior to the match. On every venue in this country this three week period is as long as can reasonably be expected for conditions to prevail.

Even then, several factors can bring changes, such as weed-cutting, late-spawning fish, seasonal baits such as hemp and tares, and even frosts which can come as early as August. These are often killer-type frosts, for the simple reason that they are exceptional, and have a more drastic effect than when they are more normally expected.

As can be envisaged, some of these developments come overnight, and teams must be on their guard to make last minute adjustments to plans in order to cover such eventualities. The three-week practice period must be unselfishly set aside by the team members. We tend to think that one match at the venue prior to the big event is often enough, but the desired amount of practice has no bounds. Because of bookings on the water, which at national venues will be unquestionably high, this practice is best done at midweek and it means that anglers must suffer some inconvenience. However, it is vitally important that the full team should be in attendance at these sessions. The final work-out should be at the end of the practice programme so that all methods and ideas learned during practice can be tried out under match conditions.

Travelling to the match can be a vital affair. We consider it well worth while to make the journey on the same day as the contest for the simple reason that bait, a high priority on the day, arrives in prime condition. Although very nice, overnight stays at hotels never lend themselves to the serious match angler's demands and, very often, bait is found to be very warm and in poor quality the next morning. If the main bait is caster, then the effect can be even more drastic.

When a full campaign at national level has been completed, other team events will come so much easier if the same formula is applied.

As mentioned earlier, discipline is a key factor, and, if a team is fortunate in achieving success, then this matter of discipline is so much easier. But, if successes are to be repeated, there can be no let-up in intensity of effort. There is no such thing as an easy team event.

18 Some Major Team Events

For most match anglers the ultimate goal is a place in the National Championship line-up. But, for a select few, the sights are aimed even higher—they envisage being included in the England team for the World Championship. Obviously, on numerical considerations alone, it is not possible for many anglers to gain this distinction. But this is an event of such importance that we cannot pass on without asking the reader to share a few moments with us discussing the world event.

In terms of reaching team perfection, the World Championship is probably the most difficult, by virtue of the method of team selection. The team manager has the responsibility of bringing together six anglers and, if possible, knitting them into a powerful match-winning unit. Though it is perhaps easier to develop a team of six, rather than an outfit twelve-strong, it does take something like four or five years for a squad of twelve anglers to reach the standard necessary to compete successfully in current team events.

On this basis, therefore, it is pretty clear that the present practice of constantly changing the team by two or three substitutions each year, representing something like a 50 per cent turnover, is just not the way to produce a winning combination. In the case of a twelve-strong National Championship team, such a scale of replacement would be tantamount to disaster.

Even to a match angler with vast experience, the World Championship is very much a one-off event in terms of the strangeness of the rules, not easily associated with the regulations in Britain, and, in fact, not even understood. Tactics, too, are vastly different from those an English angler is normally used to, and the short duration of the match—three hours—obviously does not lend itself to getting acclimatized quickly.

Bearing in mind these facts alone, it is reasonable to suggest that an angler, given a second consecutive chance in the team, would be in a far superior frame of mind to one fishing the match for the first time. We feel that this is something which has not so far been recognized. A competitor making his first appearance in the World Championship enters the match with a great deal of apprehension. To a degree that is unfounded, but, obviously, realization of this can only be gained by actually fishing the contest. This is why the advantages are enormous to the angler given a second try.

When the England team fish the match, it is almost invariably the case that it is the first time they have seen the match length, let alone fished it. No one can be blamed for this because, simply, the funds are not available for lengthy practice work-outs in foreign countries. But it would seem that if a serious attempt to win the match is to be made (up until 1976 England's best performance was in finishing runners-up) we must get our priorities right and funds must be forthcoming.

The World Championship is a match of atmosphere, fished in front of vast crowds of anything up to 20,000 spectators. Because of the strong Continental entry, the whole format of the match varies greatly from English standards, none more so than at the start of the match. Contrary to the slower English approach, the Continentals believe in getting off to a flying start! A main contributing factor to this is the unique rule applicable overseas which allows a five-minute pre-baiting period. This results in the Continental competitors unloading some 80 per cent or so of their feed into the swims before even a hook is cast! And, invariably, the catch rate starts at top level and tapers down throughout the match, exactly opposite to that of the English angler, who usually paces himself to reach peak performance in the later stages of a contest.

Perhaps this makes it easier to understand our suggestion about a second chance. Just imagine the mental condition of an angler when confronted with a pre-baiting period for the first time in his life. From experience, we can say that a bit of sound advice in this period of time would be more than welcome. The English competitor has been subjected to the most disrupting start to a match he has ever had to face. Back at home, if such an occurrence took place he would be off his creel and 'sorting out' the anglers on each side of him for ruining his chances. But, in the world match, he musk pick himself up and set about putting himself in a position to catch fish.

In all spheres of match angling it is always sound advice for an angler to do his own thing. To follow any other team or individual can only lead to being second best. The World Championship competitor must call on nerves of steel to see him through the first half of the three-hour event, before reaching the period when English anglers habitually reveal their best form—the closing stages. Among competitors who have fished in the event, it is no secret that if it were a four- or five-hour match, it would be a terrific advantage to the English side.

The resulting system is by points—one for every fish caught, plus an additional point per gram of fish weighed in. It is obvious that some teams will set their sights on small fish, and these are often caught at an alarming rate by the Continentals, which adds even more pressure on the English angler. He must pursue his home tactics of catching the larger samples if the coveted title is ever to end up on British shores.

While the World Championship match itself is accompanied by much pageantry and flag-raising, it is not to be compared with that which surrounds the after-match presentation. Both authors have been on the rostrum as members of an England team and it is something to be looked back upon with much pride, and the realization that this was a very special day. Add to this a banquet lasting for something like seven hours, and in some cases extending to seventeen courses, and it can be appreciated why to be a competitor in this world clash is the final bit of glory in a match angler's career.

We turn now to the National Championship which we have both fished for many years under both the weight and points systems. One notion which should be squashed at the outset is that there is no atmosphere in the 1st Division Championship since it has been decided on a points basis. As members of the winning team on more than one occasion since the changeover, we can categorically say that this is definitely not the case.

As has been described in a previous chapter, the National demands more time and work than any other contest. But, to savour the atmosphere on National day, and, possibly, share in the success, makes it all worthwhile.

Until an angler has competed in a National, it will be difficult for him to believe that there are so many hours in a day. The average National day starts at 4 am and ends around midnight. On rare occasions we have been known to fish the next day, but only when committed to a fixture. Otherwise, it is always a day off.

A typical National Championship day starts with the coach ride to the venue—we always use a coach because it ensures that all members of the team arrive safely. On disembarking at the match HQ, it is usually found that this has been impeccably thought out, and the atmosphere can be felt immediately. The tannoy system injects urgency into competitors and officials alike, and there are people everywhere. Our first call is usually to the bookmaker to check that team and individual bets are in order. And while here it is worth noticing the odds of some of the teams who are considered a threat, as this often reflects on an angler's confidence.

The draw is always at 8 am and, invariably, fancied peg numbers have been worked out by the pundits. Though looking back over past Nationals, not very much consistency can be drawn from these predictions, yet they always seem to be important on the day, and everyone thinks it is vital to be drawn among them.

The team captain makes the draw, and this is followed by the most important discussion of the campaign. It involves a quick, but accurate, rundown of the sections and it results in each member of the squad setting off for his peg armed with the knowledge of eleven other brains. On the journey to the section, this information will be churned over in his head. This is a good preoccupation because the one place where limitless bags of fish are 'caught' is on a National coach on its way to the section. Coming back, it might be a different story!

On arriving at his swim, a quick look on each side of him will familiarize the competitor with the immediate opposition.

136

At this stage, on a day motivated by comradeship and team sense, he will feel isolated and very much alone.

However, this feeling soon fades when the maroon signals the start, and the job in hand becomes the major factor. An early fish is much sought after in the National because it not only eliminates the dreaded 'dry net', something to be avoided at all costs in a points match, it also gives a sense of security, and a settling-down period then ensues.

Until the official finishing time of 4 pm, the experienced angler will find the match similar to other events in which he competes. But then fantasy again takes over. Competitors are not allowed to speak to anyone during the match, apart, per-haps, from a steward, and, when the silence is lifted, countless rumours fly around. However, these are nothing compared to those circulating back at HQ. For instance, it will be appreciated that, in a National of twelve sections, it is only possible to have that many section winners. Yet we have still to attend a National

Ken Giles with his fine catch of bream and roach scaling a massive 110lb which won the 1975 Woodbine Challenge title in Denmark

when the total number of section wins claimed by the various teams does not spiral to something like thirty, even forty!

However, it all contributes to an exciting day, highlighted by the announcement of the results some two hours or so after the end of the fishing. And, under the points system, it would take a very brave man to stick his neck out and predict the winning side. Having been members of a winning team more than once we can both honestly say that we have been very very relieved on hearing the result announced in our favour.

It remains only for us to say that we hope the information and guidance which we have tried to pass on in this book will enable the reader to obtain immeasurable enjoyment from his fishing, and at the same time reach a satisfying standard of success.

Acknowledgements

We would like to thank Gordon Holland for his help in compiling the book and John Sheward for the illustrations; also our families and friends for their support.

All anglers learn from fellow fishermen and we are very grateful to all of them, but we would particularly like to mention *Matchfishing* by Ivan Marks and John Godwin (Pelham Books, 1975) and *World Class Match Fishing* by Kevin Ashurst (Cassell, 1977). It goes without saying that all of us have learned much from Richard Walker's classic *Still-Water Angling* (David & Charles, new revised edition 1975).

Index

Page numbers in italic denote illustration